Four Months Lost

by
Richard Digance

Tears of laughter
Tears of pain
Tears of joy
As we meet up again

This is a boring book, written by a bored person
at a very boring time

About the author

Richard Digance is one of the vulnerable over-70s trying to survive the modern world and the problems it throws at us all. At such a testing time he returned to his first love of writing as the world of live theatre brought down its final curtain for a while.

After 11 years of television and 20 years of radio shows, he turned his back on the showbiz industry to return to his first love of writing and music. He was never one to live in the bright lights, choosing to settle in the quiet of the Wiltshire countryside. He built a recording studio where he composes reams of incidental music for film and television and he composed the music and songs for the audio book of Bill Bryson's best-selling book, The Road To Little Dribbling.

Richard was one of the great folk entertainers of the 70's along with Billy Connolly, Max Boyce and Mike Harding. His evergreen career has been acknowledged through numerous awards within both the music and entertainment industries, from a BAFTA Nomination as a television entertainer to a Gold Award from The British Academy of Composers and Songwriters in 2003. His first award was a Sony for the radio documentary Dying for a Drink.

He has supported, amongst many others, Steve Martin in the USA and Robin Williams at the London Palladium and is one of a few folk-singers to be included in the Virgin Anthology of Songwriters for his important contribution to British comedy song-writing.

Richard was born in West Ham, London in 1949, the third child of Doris Digance, a sweet-factory worker, and Len Digance, a lorry driver for Ford Motor Company in Dagenham, Essex. His earliest ambition was to be a professional footballer, but after an injury that put paid to that idea, music and writing became his life after a somewhat late start.

He attended college in Glasgow and that's where and when the green light came on. His first media attention came with the BBC, where he originally worked with satirist Bernard Braden and proudly even wrote for Basil Brush.

He joined Capital Radio, London in 1978 and presented Britain's first ever folk programme on commercial radio.

His book, The Animal Alphabet, has been featured in 14 countries as a teaching aid for the English language including;

Fearon Teacher Aids Series, Grades 4-6, Illinois, USA
Canadian Ministry of Education-The British Columbia Foundation Skills Assessment, Vancouver Canada
Oxford University Press Anthology of Verse, book 5
The New Comprehensive Strategies 1-5, Book 3, The West Indies
People For The Ethical Treatment of Animals (PETA) Foundation, London
The Animal Alphabet, BBC series
Western Australia Learning Aids

New Language For Learners, Form 1, Swaziland
April 2015- The English Genie Course, book 6, India

Whilst others came and went Richard continued to perform his unique shows of songs, rhymes and stories in a way that has been admired by the industry and the public alike. His one-man shows have taken him around the world, and his writing skills have resulted in numerous books, plays and film-scripts.

During these uncertain times Richard has concentrated purely on his writing as opposed to performance, creating a discipline of daily sessions at the computer.

Contents

The Introduction

I have been a naughty boy. I have reached a vulnerable age that I shouldn't have been allowed to reach and therefore I can't go out. The last time I was punished in such a manner must have been sixty-five years ago when I hadn't tidied my bedroom. As I write, my bedroom is still in a state and so maybe I deserve everything that's coming my way. Yes, I have been a very naughty boy and am confined to barracks due to a particularly dangerous situation I wasn't expecting, none of us were expecting. We have an unwelcome visitor who doesn't seem to want to go away, reminiscent of a boring aunt who used to visit our house every Sunday on her way home from church when I was a child. It's been nearly four months now and, although remaining healthy, fingers crossed, I'm going round the proverbial twist.

I believe tears of laughter must fall along with tears of pain, until we all experience the tears of joy that may, one day, roll down our cheeks.

This is my attempt at keeping something that couldn't possible have written by anyone not as old as myself. It's a kind of odd diary, along with trips down Memory Lane to compensate for my inability right now to walk along a high street. The plan is to make myself smile in adversity and I hope it makes you smile too.

I have dusted down and revisited all the jigsaws in my home. I have even forgiven some with pieces missing. I finished them all, the complete ones at least, with the exception of John Constable's Haywain, a beautiful painting of mainly dark trees and even darker green leaves. Cheers John! I gave up after I had pieced together Willy Lott's Cottage. Thank god the old boy painted it white. In all fairness I doubt if Constable thought for one moment his celebrated painting would end up in a thousand pieces, like some shattered tea-service. If I had been him and thought that, I wouldn't have bothered getting out my paints in the first place and carried on working for my dad at Flatford Mill.

I have rubbed the numbers off my playing cards by rigorous shuffling before endless games of Patience and I've beaten myself at Scrabble, not really a game for one, more evenings than I care to remember. At least I keep winning and that makes a nice change. Even though I'm playing on my own I still reach into the velvet bag to take more letters, my eyes looking up at the ceiling as a visual confirmation I am not cheating. Oh yes, I really am going round the twist.

So what do you do when you can't go anywhere or meet up with anyone? You fancy yourself as a bit of an author, so you decide to write a book. It's a crazy idea, I know that, but that's exactly what I decided to do and here it is. At this early point I cannot say how many pages this attempt will contain or if it will ever see the light of day, a bit like myself at this precise moment in time. To be honest, I don't really care. The sole object of this literary attempt is to stay sane at a time when insanity is ruling the world.

Most aspiring authors are young, well-educated intellects who fancy their chances of creating a best-seller instead of getting a proper job. People of my age would never entertain such a possibility, such an achievement, what with the possession of a fading memory and a typewriter somewhere up in the attic. We would be laughed out the door of a book publisher, quite understandably so, but this a book that could only be written by someone far too old to have even bothered in the first place. It is not so much a story but more a comparison between days of simple innocence that ended with us fighting for our lives against a most unwelcome guest to our shores. I must type slowly, with assured discipline, as my bottle of Tippex dried out about twenty years ago.

This is my attempt to smile in the face of adversity, an almost impossible attempt as World War Three continues, a war we are all afraid of losing. In the last war brave folk from my industry rallied to the cause, performing for the troops at various outposts and battle hotspots, singing songs, performing silly sketches and telling jokes to soldiers who hadn't laughed for months, if not years. They performed in the open-air in deserts, in makeshift tents and on the back of army trucks. It was all about keeping spirits up and this is my attempt to do the same. Every one of us are soldiers fighting a faceless army right now and during this enforced lockdown I can but try to bring the feintest of smiles to say many worried faces who have raised their drawbridges.

As we approach summer it is so strange that the smell of disinfectant, bleach and hand-wash has outweighed the smell of beautiful flowers coming into full bloom and I'm as confused as you are. Even little children are washing their hands half a dozen times a day and white van delivery drivers are suddenly the angels of the road. None of us were expecting a year like this, twelve months that would be revisited in history books forever.

I was caught unawares when, as an old man, I was instructed to stay at home by politicians because I was over seventy years of age and a medical burden to the nation. Yes, I had crossed that line into worthless territory and so it became the time to lock myself away until further notice, whether I wanted to or not. That's exactly what happened to me only a few months ago.

I abided by the rules as two weeks without meeting up with anyone seemed bearable at first. Yet, as the imposed lockdown has grown ever longer, I have become more bored and frustrated, no longer celebrating the fact I have reached an age so many of my friends and relatives never saw. If my health should hit the rocks I can have a quick chat on the phone with my doctor, assuming the surgery receptionist considers me a relevant case and not a waste of time. I just hope and pray I stay healthy in body, if not mind. That part of me has always been questionable if I'm honest.

I haven't seen my children for what seems an eternity and I missed the birthday of one of my grandchildren. I have taken to growing my own vegetables rather than the alternative of becoming one myself.

Finding more things to occupy my mind has become an increasingly arduous chore. Having said that I never got round to tidying my bedroom, or even my spare bedroom under the current circumstances, little point what with social distancing. Maybe it smacked of a kind of protest that took me back to that time when my parents ordered the same kind of imprisonment upon me. I used to love being sent to my room. It allowed me to play games without interruptions from the rest of my family. This is oh so different.

Through it all I have longed to get out and wander around the shops again, to bring normality back to my abnormal existence. I've never been one for window shopping, apart from a particular weekend I spent in Amsterdam on a stag weekend, but that is another story, yet I feel a walk around the shops would do me the world of good right now. Sadly, it isn't going to happen for quite a while.

Nothing much has changed over the last few months and I still feel the same hopeless creature I was when news first broke of the impending Third World War against an unknown, faceless enemy.

The other day I even had an urge to meet up with horrible people I can't stand. However, I changed my mind when I retrieved my old Filofax from the sideboard and went through my contacts of the past. It turned out most had died years ago, even though I had continued to send them Christmas cards, such a waste of postage, so I returned to my crazy idea of writing a book. That's the introduction over and done with. Now I need to ponder upon the content of my attempt.

So many people are falling victim to the enemy, many others already have, those who will sadly not make it through to the other side. I feel the fear of uncertainty and I need to build this distraction in my head and plough on with my life, best I can. It may help. It may help you too. Please join me.

Chapter One – Food For Thought

Let's start at the very beginning, a very good place to start according to that corny musical, The Sound of Music.

I never thought there would ever come a time in my life when food shopping would be a strategic, covert operation exercised with a military precision that would have raised the eyebrows of Sir Winston Churchill. Neither did I think I would be writing this at a time when the modern world no longer made any sense to me either. My brain is more muddled than usual and that's saying something. I'm trying to make sense of this world, we all are, and the more questions I ask myself the fewer answers I seem able to come up with. I'm usually quite good at quizzes, but right now I don't even understand the questions. It's like watching University Challenge in Cantonese.

The goalposts in the game of life haven't just been moved, they've been taken down and slung on the bonfire. None of us know what is waiting for us around the corner and, equally, none of us know what will happen to the friendly shop on that very corner. I never dreamed there would be conflict in the supermarket aisles at a level way beyond football hooliganism. I wasn't expecting any of this and neither, dear reader, were you.

What do I write about? That's always a head-banging, mind-boggling mountain to climb and, as I ponder on the various options, I keep being attracted to the matter of food shopping. I can now imagine you scratching your head and wondering why as mine has been severely scratched too. It has consumed us all, no pun intended, seeming to be all that anyone is talking or thinking about, a subject of great interest to us all. We all have to eat and most of us, we lucky ones at least who haven't yet burnt out savings, are eating more than usual out of total boredom. On the other side of the coin there are those who are struggling to put bread on the table for their children. The one thing we all share is hope, the hope that one day things will return to normal. We are smiling to ourselves and laughing with our loved ones, trying to convince one and all that everything will turn out ok in the end.

It takes fifteen face muscles to laugh and far fewer to cry. The zygomatic muscle is the main one that raises the upper lip, the stiff upper lip that we are all trying to keep right now. Those fifteen muscles haven't been that busy for months and I think it's time they were stimulated.

So, pondering for a day or two whilst wondering why none of the vegetables I'd planted in my brand new vegetable garden had bothered to show their miserable faces, I seem to be lumbered with food shopping as the subject matter. I can't think of any story that involves dragons or dinosaurs. I can't imagine a magical kingdom that hides a golden treasure waiting to be found. I've never been romantic enough to write words that would send your heart pounding in a moment of ecstasy. I'm not a proud parent who has written the next blockbuster for their children, sending their attempt to numbers of publishers who add it to the pile of other proud works of parents. It's strange how every mum, as soon as they have given birth for the first time, think they can rival Beatrix Potter for bedtime stories. It's equally odd how every dad can suddenly write super-hero stories instead of watching the football on television.

The only thing in my head as I sit down to write at this very moment is how I can get hold of some food to stop my tummy rumbling and bring some excitement back into my life. The subject matter has staked its claim, it has been defined for me, and I'm certainly not in a position to argue. Food shopping it is then, more a meal-time story than a bedtime story.

I've almost forgotten what such shopping is, but I shall dig deep into my memory cells and try to rekindle those times of freedom when I could buy a loaf of bread without standing in a queue for two hours, forced to be six feet from other shoppers who I didn't particularly want to make conversation with anyway, being bossed around by some supermarket employee who has suddenly been granted a power way beyond their station, to such an extent that I need to show some sort of identification. Identification used to be a means of proving you are not too young to acquire things like alcohol, cigarettes and magazines of naked women, but now the tables have turned and it's a means of proving I'm so old I have my own rickety queue to join. Those supermarket employees really mean business, another few months of this and they'll be armed with machine guns. Under normal circumstances that would have sounded utterly ridiculous, but nothing is ridiculous anymore. Ridicule and confusion is now the norm in a world spinning precariously on its wobbly axis.

My first ever job when I left school involved stacking shelves at a Safeway supermarket and if I had known how dominant and powerful I would have become, like some mercenary soldier working undercover for the government, I would have probably stuck with it. I stupidly moved on as I entered the world of creativity. Perhaps I would have become the power junkie I never became. Maybe I would have been an aggressive person instead of the laid-back hippie that describes the way I have lived my life for so many years. I seem to have adopted a stranger jealousy regarding the supermarket workers.

Only yesterday the Steve Martin movie, Trains, Planes and Automobiles came into my head and I realised what a mess we were all in as I came to the conclusion that all three were no longer a means of transport. The train service has come off the rails, there are no planes in the sky and cars passing by are about as rare as rocking-horse poo. Watching that film would add even more strands of jealousy to my poor soul. I am stuck indoors and I'm suddenly visiting the kitchen cupboard more times than is good for my health, but at least I'm stocked up. When I say I'm stuck indoors I mean I'm well and truly stuck indoors, more fixed than any amount of super-glue tubes could stick me to anything.

Thinking back, I have undertaken my fair number of food shops in my time, starting with a list of groceries compiled by my mother when I was knee high to a grasshopper. I was always allowed to keep the change, a fact that expanded my interest in shoplifting, a skill that would ensure my piggy-bank would burst at the seams with a multitude of coins the china pig wasn't ever expecting to swallow. I took no prisoners as, I have to confess, it was far too great a temptation for one so young. Yeah, I hold my hands up to such a criminal activity of so long ago, but I thankfully grew out of the shoplifting habit once I had secured my third Rolex watch, so no harm was done. Surely they can't come round and arrest me after all these years? To complete my confessions of criminality I also have a library book I never returned and suddenly I now have a pang of guilt passing through my veins as I think how much I must owe my former local library after fifty years. I just can't imagine having to sell my house to pay a library book fine, yet, as I mentioned, ridiculous is now the norm, so I'm expecting a legal letter to drop through the letterbox any time. I love letters from solicitors, they're a great way of starting bonfires.

Looking at a watch? I haven't bothered for months now. I don't have any idea what day it is, let alone the hour. There is no such thing as a weekend anymore as every day that passes is identical to the one before. Do you remember weekends? Weekends were days you looked forward to, time to indulge in your hobbies and meet up with your family and friends. A Sunday happened the other day. It used to be called a day of rest until every day of the week became a day of rest. It passed by and I never noticed.

There were weekend breaks when you could get away somewhere for a change of scenery. It used to be a time to do things you had put off until the two days came and for some lucky people there were dirty weekends too, in my case a distant memory of so long ago I can't remember what they entailed. The last time I had a dirty weekend I was on my own, although it did involve more than the usual quantities of moaning and groaning as I'd slipped a disc in my back and I couldn't wash as I was bed-bound. There were no red roses or champagne, just a few painkillers every four hours. At least I spent the weekend in bed and so it counts as a dirty weekend in some kind of way.

I only know summer is on its way as the sun has been shining for days on end, fuelling the prospect of burnt skin and a hose-pipe ban in a month or two despite the dreadful floods that came before.

Every living person learnt the art of food-shopping at an early age, it being expected of us all by lazy parents who couldn't be bothered to go shopping themselves and I was no exception. In my own personal case there was never any getting away from the compulsory chore as my parents were five times bigger than me, ten times if you mould them together as a united threat, so it became apparent at an early age it would be a battle I would never have won, not dissimilar to how so many of us are feeling right now.

The food shop was as vital a part of my growing up as learning to ride a bicycle or gaining free admission into the local cinema by climbing through a gents' toilet window at the back of the building. I must admit I once tried to climb in through the ladies and got myself in a bit of a tangle, thus missing the first twenty-minutes of The Lone Ranger.

Running errands for mums and dads became something we all grew out of, probably due to boredom, as we came of age and our parents stopped bossing us around, or so I thought. I never expected the world to change so dramatically in my own lifetime, and I do mean dramatic, proven by the fact I've just ordered a jar of Marmite online and like many others I'm not even struck on the stuff. Desperate times indeed. I'm quite proud of myself that I never subjected my own children to such miserable duties as family shopping. I couldn't bring myself to such a thing as times had changed so much since the early days of my own life. Besides, it would have been far too difficult for my own siblings to gather up the shopping whilst clutching their mobile phones, bottles of spring water, Play Stations and copious number of Beanie Babies. As a father I have always been more than happy to do the food shop myself. My own father, however, never saw it that way.

Going down the shops, from early age to older, was as easy as riding the aforementioned bike or opening a birthday card. It would never compare in terms of difficulty with trying to remove a chocolate cup-cake from its foil casing without leaving half the top layer behind on the wrapper. Now that really was a tricky little number. I still recall the feeling of defeat and unworthiness every time that happened to me. It, food shopping and not opening chocolate cup-cakes, would never be any more demanding than that, surely not. Wrong!

Really, really old people, well past their sell-by dates and lucky to be alive, could stumble to a shop with arched back and walking stick to buy a loaf of bread or a lump of cheese, so it never bothered me that it may well become a task beyond my own physical capabilities in years to come, but I anticipated its arrival much further down the line and not imminently. Even older, dusty specimens, if they still existed, could limp even slower to a shop, forget what they went there for in the first place and limp back home again holding an empty basket and scratching their heads. There were no restrictions a few months ago. They could go wherever they could, whenever they could, at a snail's speed that suited their frail bodies. If things went wrong there was always an ambulance to help them complete their journey with sirens blaring and blue lights flashing. They were respected sages of the community who didn't deserve to share the feeling of being surplus to requirements.

Against my own wishes I seem to have joined that category over the last couple of months and it doesn't rest easily. Come to think of it, I'm not resting too easily myself at the moment, waking up in the middle of the night, hoping all this is a bad dream, only to discover it isn't. This is a real nightmare that's really happening, scary enough to prevent me turning over, immersing myself under the duvet and going back to sleep. I think of other far less fortunate, lying in their hospital beds, wishing much the same thing. At least I can get up and make myself a cup tea. At least tomorrow I can sit in the garden and listen to the birds singing, the chirpy little things being completely oblivious to what we humans are going through. The lucky things for birds is none of them are over seventy years of age, their youth allowing them to fly about as and when they wish without fear of breaking any rules. A robin or a sparrow has little chance of outliving a tortoise, I doubt if any of them have ever lived to see sixty-five let alone seventy. They can find solace in the fact they live longer than the poor mayfly. Everything lives longer than the one-day life of a mayfly. What if it rains? They're not even around long enough to have a birthday, just as well as presents would be a problem. No diaries or tickets to see a show. Yes, the lifespan of birds that keep me company at the moment is wedged somewhere between the giant tortoise and the lowly mayfly, yet here am I suffering persecution for the age I have reached. I feel I should be celebrating such a landmark and not hiding away like some unwanted

Christmas presents. My new garden chums would swap
their lifespans with mine any day, unlike the mayfly who
couldn't swap anything any day as they wouldn't be
around long enough.
Maurice the Mayfly was born on a Sunday.
Sadly for Maurice he'd snuffed it by Monday.
One minute happily flitting about,
next minute in the gob of an ugly old trout.

Though Maurice was never one for complaining
he wasn't too pleased when he saw it was raining.
He decided to make the best of his day,
to travel the world and then have it away.

Whilst up in the air he met a brown moth
who'd developed a rather nasty old cough
and although a rather pathetic suggestion
Maurice asked if a grope was out of the question

'I don't really know about that,' said the Moth.
'I'm not really up to having it off,
but I'll show you the spot where the bees all hang out
by all accounts bees love to put it about.'

'Ignore black and yellow coats,' said the Moth,
'One wink of an eye they'll soon have them off.
They know your life's just one day, not forever,
they won't talk about marriage or living together.'

The Moth and Maurice flew down to a tree

where Maurice met a rather attractive Queen Bee.
When she undid her fur she was surprisingly thin
and to be honest, she was covered in hard scaly skin.

Maurice said although I love you to bits
do you know any friends who have got bigger tits?
By this the Queen Bee felt rather put out
so she recommended Theresa, a dodgy old trout.

'Theresa that hurts, poor Maurice moaned.
'On second thoughts, no it doesn't,' he groaned.
With every suck and every blow
Maurice cried 'God, what a great way to go!'

Maurice the Mayfly was a most content chappie.
He died the next day, satisfied...really happy.
Not one double glazing salesman he saw.
Not a single Jehovah knocked on his door.

No one asked to tarmac his drive.
No one sold him a pension while he was alive.
He never bought a time-share nor through his door.
He never won a Reader's Digest Prize Draw.

He never had to book up to see Riverdance.
Cup Final Tickets? He gave not a glance.
Maurice the Mayfly lived for just one day.
And despite that, he had a great life I would say.

I now feel grateful for being who I am as I prepare myself for an ease of these restrictions so I can go about my life, albeit in a slow way that suits my aching bones.

Oh yes, I could stumble as well as the next man and I often did as, when a partying student, I navigated my way back to my halls of residence with eyes that saw nothing and legs as strong as a pair of rubber bands. Nothing would stop me then and I stupidly presumed nothing would stop me now as I became very senior in my years. Many's the time I locked myself in self-isolation as my ceiling spun round above my head. Ah, the times I would return to our student flat after a zig-zag stumble, go to my room, and convince myself that I would jump on the bed the next time it circled close to me. A couple of days in bed and I would need to use all the experience I had gathered in my youth to get to a shop to get hold of some spaghetti and another packet of aspirins.

We all embraced the art of food shopping through its various forms and decades as we grew older and wiser. From the running of errands for parents and neighbours and onwards to the fending off of starvation and hangovers at college until the aspirins kicked in. Onwards once more to responsible adulthood and family supplies by the trolly-load, then, eventually, for so many of us, online shopping when we couldn't be bothered to rip our faces away from computer screens or mobile phones. It became an art-form in all its various styles as we all found our favourite ways of filling cupboards, fridges and freezers which in turn filled our stomachs. I, for one, knew what I was doing and how I wanted to do it with not so much as a second thought that I would ever die of starvation.

My childhood shopping errands remain ingrained and I suppose that's another reason why I never bothered to pass the burden onto my own children. There were always more important things to think about in my life to be honest, anything seemed more important. Shopping online has never appealed to me much. I just go to the shop, buy a few bits and pieces and come home again. How simple does that sound? It is simple, it doesn't just sound it. How can simplicity become a difficulty, even an impossibility, in such a short space of time? I'm trying to book a shop delivery slot online and it seems all the vans are booked up for weeks. I try another store and my Internet starts playing up.

Before I go any further it is only right and proper to be grateful and spare a thought for those who would welcome a food shop in its simplest form and not just third-world countries, I hasten to add. There are struggling people living in my own country who, even in this modern, decadent nation, search through food banks for various items donated by those who are better off. There is no stereotyping anymore either as we are not just talking of those who don't get up in the morning and go to work, certainly not. The new sector of desperation includes schoolteachers, nurses and caring staff, strangely all the occupations we rely upon to save our lives ever since the nasty enemy took control. Suddenly, those troubled and struggling people have become the most important people in the whole world, ironically people who sometimes struggle to undertake food shops of their own. It's all such a crazy state of affairs that gets crazier by the day. I lost a few days in an alcoholic haze at college, but never three or four months before. I'm feeling sorry for myself when I shouldn't be feeling sorry for myself.

There are so many starving people in the world, so many children who have such an unhealthy start to their short lives, it would be criminal of me not to recognise their plight and feel the deepest sympathy at this time. Please do not think bad of me for not making light of my own issues that came to the fore at a time in my life when I had the whole damn thing mastered with not so much as a second thought. I accept I have been one of the lucky ones, born into a blessed, civilised society that never went without, but I feel I still have the right to grumble to get things off my chest. I am a pensioner and all pensioners like to moan and be miserable. This enforced retirement certainly wasn't on my bucket list.

I never realised how important my own food shopping expeditions would become until such a luxury had been taken from me by that unwelcome visitor to our shores in the shape of a nasty thing that would shake the planet to its unsteady roots. No longer would shopping be a simple, uncomplicated necessity that none of us particularly enjoyed. It had become a full-scale retaliation against the situation we all found ourselves in. The whole game had become bedecked with greed and selfish self-survival, even warfare, as man fought fellow man in open combat for a two-pound bag of flour or a wad of pasta they didn't particularly want to buy in the first place. Supermarkets were suddenly selling more toilet-rolls than there were arses, along with hand-washing lotions that had stood on supermarket shelves for months, completely ignored by those who had suddenly realised their importance and rushed to the aisles, pushing others out of the way. The charge of the fight brigade had well and truly begun up and down the country.

All of a sudden we were shopping with masks over our mouths, handling goods with plastic gloves and keeping our distance from other shoppers who also looked dressed for a shift in an operating theatre. The worst possible nightmare had come true and there was no way we would wake up in the morning, just like I had before and realise it had just been that bad dream I described earlier. It really was happening and getting worse by the day. Have you ever gone to bed and wished for a nightmare not as bad as the one you had experienced during the day? I'm sure none of us had felt that before, but many of us have done exactly that recently. It's a weird feeling of hopelessness that overtakes you.

In a matter of a few short weeks, every technique we had individually developed over the years had been thrown out of the window as the military campaign for our stomachs intensified. Choices of food became limited, choices of how get hold of the food became even more limited and strict shopping rules had to be obeyed for the first time in our lives. Nobody felt too sure how long it would last or if the world would ever be the same again. There was certainly doubt in my own mind and I found the whole scenario scary, as did most people. That was the nightmare I wanted to escape from as I turned over in my bed. As the weeks have passed into months nothing much has changed and I still don't understand how all this came to be, but I'm still doing as I am told and living the life of an over-aged hermit.

I feel my entire lifestyle, my future, has been slung into the laps of politicians who don't exactly come out of most things with flying colours. On this dreadful occasion there are no flying colours at all, more a white flag of surrender as they flap around giving contradictory updates that make little sense. I have never trusted any of them anyway as they seem to be an opportunistic bunch incapable of giving a straight answer to any question, including their date of birth. They bumble and stumble their way through press conferences with an air of bewilderment, to them and us alike, as they try to conjure up a magical plan to keep us all safe, suggestions completely different to the day before. After three months of this they are still telling me not to forget to wash my hands, something my dear old mum told me to do over half a century ago. I've always washed my hands and I think I mastered the art before most of those politicians were born.

I obviously don't include them all, but many have a track record of bending the rules to suit themselves. After all, we're talking of a mob who have given themselves three pay rises in as many years as the rest of the nation floundered in depressing austerity. Did I trust them now? No. Would you trust a politician with your life? Well, we kind of are and it doesn't rest comfortably with me. Scientists and doctors, yes, they have my utmost faith and trust, but the other lot? Make your own mind up.

Grandparents will boast that the new regulations imposed upon us are nothing compared with what they had endured for five long years during The Second World War and that cannot be denied. Back then the skint public were issued coupons that allowed them to have sugar, meat, cheese and even a tin of powdered milk. Powdered milk? Try pouring that on your cornflakes with doodlebugs flying overhead. The government of the time, or more accurately The Ministry of Food as it called itself as a means of lawful authority, encouraged everyone to grow their own vegetables, something I'm now trying myself in this current predicament. Fine for those, like me, fortunate enough to live in the countryside, but not so great for those surviving in a city. Potatoes don't grow in window-boxes the same as money doesn't grow on trees.

The whole thing back then became known as 'Dig For Victory.' Food in the 1940s became scarce and some items were not available again for many years after the war ended. Bread, for example, was rationed for a long time after the war, at a time when electric bread-making machines hadn't been invented, let alone stored away as unwanted wedding presents, only to be dusted down during this current crisis. Everyone seems to be making their own bread now and it's a luxury that only the few enjoyed in our grandparents' time. I've tried making bread myself but I can't seem to get the mixture to come out the oven in slices.

I fully respect food rations were short after the war and our grannies would have welcomed such choices afforded us today. That very thought has made me realise how fortunate I have been. I think we have all taken food shopping as an easy, but quite tedious, part of our existence and we cannot be blamed for that as it was easy and tedious in equal proportions, but on reflection, we've been blessed.

We all spent years getting it right, perfecting the art, taking full advantage of what we learnt as kids about raiding a shop and getting what we needed into a couple of carrier bags, but, all of a sudden, it has gone, all of it has gone, with a tickly cough and a high temperature. The skill, the desire, even the need has shut down as though it is an early-closing Thursday afternoon in the high street.

Delivery-van drivers are no longer described as manic motorists as they meander their way from street to street with food from shops that are otherwise closed for business. They are now the new saints of the open road who, minimum, deserve knighthoods. White van drivers are suddenly admired bastions of society as opposed to cursed villains as they race around the country like crazed animals with a valid reason. The world has been kicked in the Brussel sprouts and things seem unlikely to return to whatever normal happened to be once upon a time. The delivery drivers have answered the call in an admirable way and we all forgive them for driving whilst on their mobile phones, overtaking long queues at roadworks and generally being pains in the proverbial arses. Yes, we forgive them all that.

As the first few months of self-isolation passed the food shop had become unrecognisable to what we had all known in the past. We all became too scared to buy newspapers, even while we were still aloud to be out and about. Our boundaries of confusion and tolerance had been stretched to the limit and the stroll around the supermarket at leisure had gone forever. The press accentuated the gloom as this became the first media-fuelled illness.

On a lighter note, if there actually is one, I can't help wondering what will happen to all the single people who set forth in search of meeting a new love down the frozen food aisle, an acceptable ulterior motive for a food shop. Hugs and kisses have disappeared as fast as bottles of bleach and pasta off the shelves.

What on earth will happen to the fashion-conscious female shopper who strolls the aisles with gay abandon, mobile phone in one hand and a take-away coffee or a bottle of water in the other? Surely they must be struggling to survive such a lockdown? They have no choice but to adapt. None of us have any choice at this time of abject fear.

Despite my vast shopping experience and knowledge of the subject, due to many mounting years, I realise the time has now come to mentally revisit as many shopping trips through the years. They come and go like a scatter-gun in my head, so please excuse the darting around as my brain goes on a free-for-all ramble. I want to know if all the hours I've put into mastering such a chore has really been worth all the bother. I sense not, a depressing scenario, but everything is depressing so it's just joining the club.

As I sit here now, I haven't set foot in a shop, any shop, for well over three months. The high streets are empty, looking like cowboy towns with the townsfolk hidden away because the bandits are riding into town. Food shopping is out the window, which sounds like I am looting because I've seen thugs doing exactly that on the TV news.

It really is amazing how something so bland can be elevated to a level of grand importance, so much so that someone has even decided to write a book about it. There can be nothing so boring a subject can there? Surely no-one in their right mind would even consider thinking such pages would be of interest to anyone except the exceedingly bored? Right mind? Where did that go? Well, here is that very book and I hope you, dear reader, are exceedingly bored enough to enjoy it further. If not, I perfectly understand.

The first obstacle I had to encounter when all this began was how to continue my ritual of starting each day with The Daily Telegraph crossword. That may seem trivial, and probably is, but I have always checked the alertness of my brain each day before daring to go about my creative duties. If I fail with my crossword I choose not to attempt writing anything that would need brainpower at full steam. I have since discovered the crossword is published online, a simple statement for anyone who is computer literate but, sadly, I am not. I have now overcome such a horrendous trial which makes me feel quite proud of myself.

I lost interest in computers long ago, but the time has now come to rekindle, if you'll pardon the pun, my need to understand the contraptions that had taken over the world in the 1980s by keeping my crossword ritual going through the dark days that lay ahead. They are a one-hour oasis of calm each day.

I seem to have far more idle time in my head than usual and such a vacant area constantly sends me back to moments in my life I'd forgotten about or placed so far back in my mental filing-cabinet they were unlikely to ever surface again. Surface they have and I must admit, some of them make me smile with a feeling of contentment as I think back upon the easy days of my life.

When I was a little boy I indulged in a game we called Knockdown Ginger. I had no idea how the title came to be, but it entailed knocking on someone's front door for some unaccountable reason and then running away before they opened it. It was great fun, harmless for youngsters and downright annoying for older people. It was basically a game of 'who dares' or 'chicken' without having to run across a main road in front of buses or stand in front of a train as it sped towards you with no exceptional braking system to speak of. Knockdown Ginger disappeared in the 1950s, when everyone became bored stupid with both running and opening doors, yet a similar game came to life just a couple of months ago.

This new version of the same annoying game is called Lockdown Ginger, where people such as postal workers and delivery drivers knock on your door and run away, just as we did all those years ago. I never thought I would see the fun game ever return, but return it has. They now run away to keep us safe from harm, not to annoy us, but the principle is the same. Before the current issues I used to say Knockdown Ginger had been given the new name of Parcel Force, but now I eat my words.

Back in the day, the game had different names around Great Britain, ranging from rat-a-tat in the north of England, to cherry knocking in the south. I admit that the people of Liverpool gave it its best title, Thunder and Lightning, whereby kids thundered on the door and ran away as fast as lightning. I remember asking someone from Norfolk what they called knocking on the door and running away and the reply was knocking on the door and running away. Knockdown Ginger it was in London, where I was raised, and I just had to find its derivation before I move on to other matters.

By all accounts it comes from an 18th Century poem, Ginger, Ginger broke a winda, a rhyme if you're a Londoner like me. He hit the winda. Crack. The baker came out to give him a clout and Ginger landed on his back.

Well, they certainly knew how to write wonderful poetry back in the 18th Century did they not? No-one seems to take any literary credit for that little gem though.

The game was played in America too, but being American they had to give it their own name, so they called it Ding Dong Ditch or Nicky Nocky Nine Doors. Not as good as Knockdown Ginger. I rarely played the game myself as I knew my nosey neighbours were always looking out their windows, through their net curtains, so they would have known it was me. I used to run errands for these people. If I knocked on their doors it was to deliver a bag of sugar and collect a few pence for my trouble. I preferred to be a budding businessman than a silly little yob.

I couldn't have been more than five or six years old when my food shop training began, a chore that would come to such a dramatic halt in such a painful manner. I sense we all started out the same and in my case it started with the fish and chip shop, a vinegar-scented establishment I was sent to every Friday evening.

As I approach the next chapter I am more than grateful this project has, for a short time at least, taken my mind off the dreadful events taking place around me and the rest of the world. So many people have sadly died, struck down by a faceless army during this Third World War. So many are in hospital beds, frightened out of their lives, and so many are wondering if their lives will ever be the same again. I know my contribution is minimal.

I have said my silent farewells to two close friends, two mates with whom I've shared so many laughs and good times during my life. Their lives didn't deserve to end like this. Nobody's lives deserve to end like this. As far as our children and grandchildren are concerned, they don't deserve to start their lives like this either. With my senior years I am able to go back further than most to hunt out and reincarnate a society, a less frightened society, that never dreamt for one moment that this horrific event would occur. I find solace within my memories as they offer me some kind of respite from my daily fears as I live through The Third World War.

Our lives are in the laps of gods,
so we are here against the odds.
Our lives are torn apart and petrified.
Blessings we have counted now.
We're still here and we don't know how.

We're the survivors who reached the other side.
The day the Third World War came,
things would never be the same.
Friends we'll never see again,
lost in The Third World War.

To us all the army came,
no uniform, no shape or name.
Trillions upon trillions came to take our lives one day.
An enemy we never saw
brought to us The Third World War.
It took us by surprise and took so many lives away.

The day the Third World War came,
things would never be the same.
Friends we'll never see again,
lost in The Third World War

It picked the sickly of our fold,
then turned attentions to the old,
those who never had the strength to stand and fight.
As they joined old soldiers in the sky
with not a chance to say goodbye,
leaving us survivors, the ones who held on tight.

The day the Third World War came,
things would never be the same.
Friends we'll never see again,
lost in The Third World War.

Memories of those we lost,
those who sadly paid the cost.
Memories of those we hold most dear,
wishing they were all still here.

The day the Third World War came,
things would never be the same.
Friends we'll never see again,
lost in The Third World War.

Our lives are in the laps of gods,
so we are here against the odds.
Our lives are torn apart and petrified.
Blessings we have counted now.
We're still here and we don't know how.
We're the survivors who reached the other side.

The day the Third World War came,
things would never be the same.
Friends we'll never see again,
lost in The Third World War.

Chapter Two – The Fish and Chip Shop

I ate fish long before I knew what one looked like. I remember wondering at a very young age how they swam in the sea without heads, tails, or even fins. I'm certain I didn't really have to add 'at a very young age' to the previous sentence. It's obvious I learnt fish never lacked such physical attributes as I grew older for god's sake. I'm sure everyone who writes a book knows what a fish looks like, or at least a couple of varieties. I did warn you that my brain is acting like some scatter-gun at the moment and here is your first confirmation. The chances of writing a book with some sensible level of vocabulary would be an impossibility for anyone who didn't know cod had heads, even writers who aren't too sure if the plural of such fish is cod or cods. Hang on just a moment, the plural of haddock is haddock and yet the plural of dolphin is dolphins. What's going on? Am I really in a fit mental state to be carrying on with this literary attempt? The answer is probably no, but I'm about to give it a good go as I have nothing else to do and if this becomes a best-seller I will be in a far better position to pay my Council Tax and reduce the balances on my credit cards.

Fish and chips were a treat back in the day and, as the youngest member of the family, my job, of which

I had no choice, was to run down to the fish shop, buy the required shoal, before running back home even faster to ensure the catch was still warm enough to eat. My mother would never have managed such a hasty return, stopping to chat to other mums of the neighbourhood and admiring new-born, ugly babies in prams, to say nothing of the problems relating to her dodgy left hip or popping into to someone's house for a quick cup of tea. Fish would have been shivering on the plate by the time my dear mum had returned from such a journey.

My father would never have even bothered in the first place. A stroll to the fish and chip shop, as far as he was concerned, was totally out of the question after a hard day's work in the factory. Dad fell asleep in the armchair as soon as he got home and it took many nudges of his shoulder before he realised his dinner, presented on an old tray, a drab souvenir from Bognor Regis, was ready for consumption. It was left for all young kids to go shopping and, being the youngest as well as and the most bullied, I always knew it would be down to me as an inherited burden. I was battered as much as the fish by my older brother who happened to have a bike, unlike myself, so it would have been far easier for him to do the shop rather than me. He pulled rank and stayed indoors on Friday evenings, building his model aeroplanes. He made contribution whatsoever on Friday evening and yet he always ended up with more chips than anyone else. No wonder we never got on.

All fish looked exactly the same in the shop as they lay there in strict formation, dressed in their brown, uneven coats of something vaguely edible. Whatever they looked like when alive I had no idea. I had swum a couple of times when we were taken to the coast on a nice day out, but I'd never been joined alongside by a cod or a haddock as I splashed around with a car tyre innertube around my waist. I once trod on a disgruntled crab that painfully retaliated, but that never helped with my fish identification either.

So what exactly is or was batter, the very stuff those brown coats were made of? The word batter comes from the French word battre which means 'to beat.' It's a term that could well take me back to more stories of my brother but, no, I've long forgiven him for the fish battering and the bruising I endured. To make a batter correctly you start with flour apparently, I don't make claims to be a chef, before adding baking powder and salt, furiously stirring the three ingredients into a pulp before adding milk and a modicum of water for good measure. In the fish shop of old the batter lay festering in a huge aluminium vat. It could have been lumpy custard to the untrained eye, but I knew better. It was definitely batter, awaiting to go about its business as fish clothing.

It always struck me as an enlightening experience to watch the skilled man behind the counter as he dipped the white objects, the anonymous slices of fish, into the cooking mixture before slinging them into the bubbling cooking oil with great skill. He never allowing any batter to drip onto the shop's floor. A genius at work.

We are not talking of fresh oil here by the way. Public health and safety was still a long, cloudy way down the track which meant the oil only needed to be changed or added to as its level dropped, not unlike the sump of an old car, or if the chip shop man dropped his cigarette lighter in as he tried smoking a fag whilst coating the fish. The man never had to wear gloves or wash his hands either, he being such an important man in the area, a bastion of the neighbourhood. We simply deemed him qualified to feed us safely without questioning his levels of health. He was way beyond having to be hygienic. He owned a shop, for heaven's sake, he had to be important. He had a strange wort that resembled a tiny walnut on the end of his nose, but I don't think that affected his cleanliness as he cooked my family's dinner with great aplomb and assurance every Friday evening while my brother completed his model spitfire. He knew when the oil needed topping up, just like his father and grandfather before him. It was a skill that had been handed down through the generations and that was good enough for my family.

I hasten to add here that, above and beyond the reference to fresh oil, I use the term of just oil loosely too. I'm fairly sure the boiling mass wasn't quite what we have grown to expect in more recent times. For a start, it had a dark brown hue, not as golden as one expects to see nowadays.

My element of doubt about its well-being stems from the fact that our chip-pan at home had no oil at all, just fat or lard or whatever it was called. To cook chips at home we had to wait half an hour before the horrible congealed lump melted into liquid form before the poor chips were cremated.

I must admit I don't recall ever seeing such suspect lumps of lard in the fish and chip shop but, there again, I wasn't really looking that intently and I certainly wasn't around half an hour before the man with the grubby white apron opened his shop to the public. I never knew, thankfully I never knew.

Olive oil? Are you serious? Olive was Popeye's girlfriend, nothing more, and it remained a fair few decades away from our kitchens. It was only used by the French and Italians, two places I knew very little about other than they both had football teams, plus the fact that the French smoked ghastly smelling cigarettes, themselves smoked, and the Italians shoved more hair-cream on their heads than any other nation. Beyond that I struggled.

The fish and chip shop I went to as a child bore no resemblance to the fish and chip shop of today. There were no pies whatsoever, of any variety, no jumbo sausages, limp sausage-rolls filled with a bright pink something or other and definitely no curry sauce, exotic fish-cakes or fridges full of fizzy drinks. Yes there was, and still is, the totally pointless calendar on the wall that no-one ever looked at and a pile of wooden forks on the counter that snapped in half if you tried to dissect a chip with too much force, but, other than that, the fish and chips of different generations bore little resemblance to each other.

The fish and chip shop sold fish and chips, end of, and the bloke in charge never had a staff other than his miserable wife whom he hadn't spoken to for over five years, even though they had a four-year-old daughter. As a young kid on errand duty I never experienced strange girls serving behind the counter as they moaned to each other about their boyfriends with great volume as they served me.

They didn't wear those stupid white, rubber boots either. They were selling bits of fish not catching the damn things on a trawler in a force ten gale. White pinafores were good enough as a kind of uniform of authority, along with an ashtray by the side of the counter to ensure no fag-ends fell into the swirling bubbles. We trusted them both, Mr and Mrs Fish Shop, to deliver the goods in impeccable fashion. They had a skill that allowed them to recognise a piece of cod from a piece of haddock without them being labelled. Oh yes, the fish and chip shop proprietor and his wife were clever people alright, knowing their trade inside out, even if they didn't bother to wash their hands too often. They would definitely struggle with the regulations of today if they were still around. They didn't wear hygienic hats either. They didn't need to as the man's hair was bedded down, like layers of lasagne, with excessive Brylcreem and the woman had a ponytail that hung limply down her back. That was good enough for me as, at such a young age, they came across as upstanding pinnacles of our society.

There were four other kinds of fish written up on the board in white chalk and they were fish I never ate due to their cost. There were plaice, for example, a flatfish that cost a little more than the more regular cod and haddock and, with my family never bothering to spend more than was ever necessary, we never indulged. All fish were flat anyway by the time they left the shop, so we never thought of a plaice as such a big deal and certainly not worth spending more money on when we were saving up for a holiday.

In passing, we never bothered with pickled onions either as they looked like eyeballs stolen from a local mortuary. It could be said that pickled gherkins, although from a different part of the anatomy, could have been nicked from the same dubious establishment. It's enough to make an empty stomach churn. I have one such empty stomach at the moment and it's churning at the very thought.

Rock salmon was another variety of fish that never tasted as grand as it sounded. It wasn't salmon at all, which probably explains why. I sussed that fact at an early age because I knew salmon didn't live in rocks, they jumped over them, or tried to at least. Rock salmon was nothing more than the grand description, maybe the gran description, of the down-trodden dogfish, a scavenger that patrolled the grubby bed of The North Sea and Thames Estuary as opposed to a beautiful Scottish river that raced down from The

Highlands as clear as a bell. They were fish that hoovered up unwanted bits and pieces slung from boats or dropped by seagulls who weren't too struck on the offerings. No, graceful salmon they really were not. Dogfish look like tiny, angry sharks and their skin can cut your hands to ribbons if you pick one up during a successful fishing trip. Covered in batter, such skin would not have been spotted but our family never took the risk of such an injury due to the razor-sharp outer-coating. My dad needed his lips to roll his cigarettes and would never have risked damaging his tongue that added moisture to the cigarette paper. To my dad that would have been a health hazard. Rock salmon gave totally the wrong impression, but we were never taken in by it.

All fish are ugly, staring objects who care little about their looks and so I don't think any scruffy dogfish tried to pass itself off as a leaping salmon. It was nothing more than a name conjured up by the fish market to help get rid of fish that nobody would have eaten by choice. I suppose the same could be said for scampi, it being nothing more than a posh name for the tails of the monkfish, which only goes to show how ugly the head of monkfish must be if you have to eat their tails. What about even posher caviar, a collection of black eggs from the sturgeon? No thanks, we ate proper eggs from chickens. It was all a case of bullshit baffling brains, but we were never taken in but that either. It makes me kind of proud that I hail from such a smart family.

Basically, it seemed the oceans of the world were mostly populated with cod and haddock and that was that. At least it was until the first of The Cod Wars in 1958. I was very young and didn't understand the ins and outs of such a hostile battle on the high seas. Now much older and wiser I have worked out the obvious, the British cod attacked the Icelandic cod over something territorial and many cod were killed in action, just like any other war. Because of the fatalities far fewer cod were around to end their lives in the fish and chip shop, thus the new varieties of fish that needed to be invented for our hungry mouths. I remain convinced the wars of 1958 played a major part in the rise in popularity of the rock salmon, the rock eel and, much later, the demand for scampi. I may be of a vulnerable age, but you can see I know what I'm talking about. Sometimes it comes in handy to be old enough to remember when history didn't exist, when everything was current affairs. Yes it comes in handy to be old enough to remember when The Dead Sea wasn't even ill.

The final make of fish chalked up on the board was the skate, by far the most expensive of all, even more so than the pricey plaice. Even wrapped in batter they were a different, more stately, shape to all the others, hardly surprising as they were a different shape to the rest when they swam around at the bottom of the sea. They resembled kites we flew in the sky as kids, but obviously without the string attached. Skate were basically two giant, flapping wings with a very ugly head stuck in the middle. When I say head I'm being more than generous as they didn't really have heads, only a mouth and a pair of bulbous eyes. The only edible part of the strange looking thing were those wings and, for some reason that I cannot possibly explain, a piece of skate from the fish and chip shop came in a similar triangular shape, a smaller version of the whole fish, looking like it had been caught by Pythagoras. Even a young kid like myself could spot the difference between a rather balletic looking piece of skate and a lump of cheap cod. It stood high and proud, even though it was, as flat as a plaice in real life. Skate were the same colour as the sea- bed, allowing them to bury themselves away and lie in wait for their own dinner in total camouflage. They were also the underwater hide and seek champions year in year out, other multi-coloured entrants not really standing much of a chance.

Then there were the chips, proper chips I'm talking about, each lovingly carved by the man's wife while she listened to the radio the previous evening. There were no machines that automatically peeled and cut a potato into ten pieces. I'm talking of a time when the first washing-machines had only just appeared in the shops along with the first television sets. An automatic potato-peeler? Chips were chips and not skinny French-fries, the pathetic emaciated ones that pose like cat-walk models in fast-food shops. They were sturdy enough to handle a thunderstorm of vinegar before they were wrapped and sent packing to our homes. Yes, upon purchase the fish and the chips were rolled up in newspaper after being doused in copious amounts of that vinegar and a Siberian gust of salt. The smell lingered in our living-room for days on end, a smell that a tin of Johnsons furniture wax could not eradicate.

It wasn't unusual to unwrap the goods when you returned home, only to discover the imprint of Bobby Charlton or Sir Stanley Matthews on the arse of a piece of cod that had been wrapped in the sports pages of the Daily Mirror. It makes me wonder if those two famous footballers bought fish and chips themselves and, if so, what great names adorned the backsides of their own fish suppers.

Plain white paper was adopted by the local butcher long before the fish and chip shop caught on to the far more hygienic idea. I recall how The Daily Mirror absorbed more vinegar than news. That particular newspaper seemed to be the most popular form of wrapping, particularly where I was brought up. The chances of yours truly seeing a piece of fish covered by The Sunday Times colour supplement or The Financial Times were zero.

One of the perks of my youth was to deliver old newspapers to the shop and be given a free bag of chips in return. That was my first taste of real communism and bartering. I considered it another opportunity to start out in business, along with running errands for those neighbours, but things fell apart with the advent of plain white paper long before I had the chance to form a limited company and take on staff.

With fish and chip shops now closed, along with so many other retail outlets, I couldn't help but reflect on how much I wouldn't really miss them. I could go without. I never thought I would lovingly recall the way they were once upon a time, such establishments of my youth, and yet that's exactly what has happened. I do not lament their passing. I smile as I still see the face of the man behind the counter with his grubby apron and equally grubby plaster on the thumb he injured whilst tackling a particularly resistant backbone of a fish. I see the cigarette smoke rising from his counter like early morning mist above a Scottish stream. I still see my brother stealing half my chips because he was older than me and I see my dad smothering his dinner in brown sauce long before tomato ketchup came onto the scene. I didn't want or expect the social distancing of customers at the fish and chip shop of today. In a more general and selfish way, or perhaps that should read a more shellfish way, I didn't want pickled eggs, battered sausages, not even the varieties of burgers that were on offer and I certainly had no intention of waiting an hour in a queue to get my hands on such a feast. Social distancing for me now means social exclusion as I daily stick my head in the freezer to find alternatives.

In more recent years I'd found such shops a little scary anyway as they'd become gathering places of young people who looked mighty menacing, even if they weren't. You get to my age and all young people over the age of five and a half look menacing, weighing you up to see if you're worthy of a good mugging. Oh dear, whatever happened to the innocent days of kiss-chase and hop scotch? My friends and I never skulked around the streets looking for limping, decrepit victims with the intention of stealing their pensions.

I've now realised how harsh I have been as I've never seen young people homing in on an older person as they hung around inside the fish and chip shop. I will go even further by saying I am touched how such young people have rallied to the cause in large numbers and helped the elderly with their shopping. I can but apologise but offer the excuse that the whole, accusing world seems out of order and not just me.

My relationship with the good old fish and chip shop has come to an abrupt end, leaving me with nothing but the distant memory of a minor part of the food shop I undertook for my family. We didn't have fish and chips every Friday, maybe once a month. That particular shop has now had its chips.

I know how to slice a potato into small pieces as well as the next man or woman and I know how to cook a healthy piece of fish too, if you can class 'piece of dead fish' healthy. With such skills I can be my very own fish and chip shop whenever I need to be. To complete the image I also have a grubby apron, as grubby as all my other clothes right now.

I have seen my own children turn to the pizza delivery store rather than stay in the world of cod and chips and I can't blame them. Progress is progress. Fish are downright ugly things anyway and it can't be good to shove such ugliness down your throat. My children eat enough pizzas to topple the leaning tower of inaccurately the same name.

Time to endorse a clarification. There was a distinct difference between a fish and chip shop, the likes of which I have been describing, and just a fish shop. They weren't the same thing at all and yet, for younger readers, it is a simple error to categorise them as one. The latter was known, to give it its full title, as a wet fish shop, a name granted to such places as fishmongers used to sling buckets of water over the display and lay them in ice, a complete waste of time as they weren't about to spring back into life any time soon. The wet fish had a very distinctive smell too, of fish. Ah yes, my nose twitches as I think of that pungent aroma. I recall how it used to remind me of the seaside, or at least the seaside when the tide had ebbed away back into the deeper ocean. That smell of seaweed and damp sand wafted out the wet fish shop and into the high street where it mingled with various other fragrances from the various other shops.

There they all lay, mackerel with their heads and tails intact with shiny skin that looked like it had been painted by a child who'd run out of drawing paper. Beside them were prawns and herring that hadn't been smoked or pickled. Also on display were the two representatives of the freshwater fish community, the rainbow trout and the salmon. Any of the varieties, particularly the latter two, were far too expensive as far as my own family were concerned, thus it became a shop I never entered. Even looking through the window didn't interest me, such a shame as, if I had bothered, I would have known what intact fish looked like.

I think back now and realise it was an experience I missed out on, peering through the window at a kind of static aquarium with fish of all shapes and sizes plus crab and lobster, a veritable sea of colour and splendour to one so young. I should have embraced the wet fish shop with more gusto, I realise that now as the tide has gone out on those shops, possibly never to flow back in, a sad prophecy.

My memory will only recall with far more accuracy the other kind of shop with its amazing, explosive sound as the chips went into the fryer next to the shapeless objects floating around in their brown coats. I admit, particularly for the vegetarians reading this, it wasn't a great way to go, but is there such a thing anyway?

I haven't stood in front of a shop window of any description for three months and I would give anything right now to stand outside a fish and chip shop, or a wet fish shop if pushed, even a shop that sold rotten eggs and trousers without legs, as a means of escape from this lockdown nightmare that has drawn my life to a temporary halt. Unable to witness anything with my own eyes I only know what is happening on the high street through television or radio bulletins and I tend to take notice of fewer by the day. I sense shops are now dropping like nine-pins, but I have no idea how my personal favourites are faring or if they haven't already closed. I feel so bad for them all. I feel so helpless too, as they do too, no doubt. Who says ignorance is bliss? This experience isn't blissful in any way and I'm not ignorant of the fact.

It humbles me to think of hard-working members of our community losing their jobs and, quite possibly, their homes. For many of them a fish and chip supper has become a luxury they can no longer afford. There's no surprise I feel humbled. I think of all the fish being caught in the trawler's nets, only to be dumped back into the sea in a poor state or slung to the seagulls because the fish-markets are barely trading. The repercussions of this terrible time resound time and again as the enemy advances, no-one excluded from the perils it throws at us.

My fish and chip shop experience has now closed in so many different ways.

Chapter Three – The Grocer's Shop

Grocer Jack, grocer Jack, get off your back, go into town, don't let them down, oh no, no. I have no idea why that number one song of 1967 came into my head at this moment. It was recorded by Keith West and was bizarrely titled Excerpt From a Teenage Opera. It proved to be a bit of a con because it wasn't an excerpt from a teenage opera at all, just as well really because there aren't too many teenagers interested in opera. It was nothing more than a one-off, stand-alone song. Even the B side of the single was Theme From an Excerpt Opera by The Mark Wirtz Orchestra, a real instrumental bonus for cool kids eh? It never flexed its muscles to become a mammoth musical like Evita or Les Misérables. Anyway, I haven't got the time to discuss number-one hit records of half a century ago. Come to think of it, yes I have. How about Something Stupid by Frank and Nancy Sinatra? There really is something stupid going in our lives right now.

So, onwards and sideways to the grocer's shop, the grocers, the grocery, call it what you will. A high street shop of paramount importance. A high street of years gone by just wasn't a high street unless it had a smart grocer's shop. I never knew there were so many charities until they all started opening shops as replacements to the traditional traders.

The old-fashioned grocers had a most distinctive smell, yet I cannot for the life of me remember what it stank of. The only word I can think of that sums it all up is purity. You see, back in the good old days when high streets had shops that were open for business, shopping was a crusade of visiting various shops of various fragrances for various goods and the good old grocery shop took the biscuit. It smelt clean and welcoming, nothing like the bicycle shop two doors down that stank of oil and rubber tyres. Nobody ever bought a bike that smelt of freshly sliced ham or detergent.

The grocer's shop never had trolleys, just baskets. The shops weren't big enough to have trolleys, or certainly not more than one or two. Trolleys back then were only used for carting old people around hospitals. Nobody bought meat at the grocer's and nobody bought steak and kidney pies or tins of corned beef at the butcher's. There was a designated venue, and smell, for each designated item and that's how we went about our shopping trips, going backwards and forwards like busy bees around a jar of jam, hunting out the scents that wafted from each sop doorway.

The only thing I never quite understood was why dad bought his tobacco at the newsagents and yet he had his Exchange and Mart, a newspaper of sorts, delivered on a wet Thursday by a struggling paper-boy who broke a shoulder carrying a few dozen of the things in a giant sack as he cycled around making his deliveries in the inclement weather. Other than that singular instance it all made some kind of sense. Horses for courses as they say. You knew exactly what you wanted and what you were getting with each shop you entered. It was all part of the training we would need to undertake for our later years as we came of age and shopped for ourselves rather than for our mums and dads.

The stately grocer always wore a navy-blue apron with white stripes and most had moustaches, well at least the male variety did, with the exception of Mrs Barnard who I remember well as a kind of circus freak. They looked clean and authoritative as they stood behind their counters like guards at Buckingham Palace. No matter what you asked for they always had it in stock. There were no empty shelves like the supermarkets of today that have put so many of them out of business.

In the defence of supermarkets however, the grocer never sold pasta because nobody had ever heard of pasta, let alone know what kind of animal it was, and neither did they sell hand washing lotions. There was no need when a wholesome bar of Sunlight or Wrights Coal Tar Soap did the trick and lasted weeks. In truth, most people never washed their hands too often anyway. Kids in school never washed their hands after going to the toilet and grown-ups seldom washed their hands at lunch breaks or before handling goods. They are more rigid requirements that only seem to be important as things have become scarier.

As a young child I bathed every Sunday night, whether I was grubby or not, and that healthy routine seemed to get me through the week for many of my adolescent years. Sometimes I helped with the washing-up and the splashing around in Fairy Liquid proved to be somewhat of an added health bonus as the dirt dislodged from under my fingernails swam around in the washing-up bowl alongside the cups and saucers.

Nowadays, of course, people even wash their hair every day. How ridiculous. I can't subscribe to such an indulgence. I washed my hair four times per month and it always seemed to look ok until I lost it all in later years. As an aside, I still do not understand why bald men have to shampoo their heads every day when there's nothing sprouting out. It's nothing more than just a silly ritual that makes them feel they look better than they really do. Bald people should wear hats and save themselves some time every morning. Maybe bald people shouldn't have gone bald in the first place. They only have themselves to blame.

The shopping list for the grocer's shop was longer than most and yet it was still the responsibility of me, as a young child, to go to the shop and ask for the items my mother had written down in her best handwriting. Do you remember being told to write something in your best handwriting? As if there was a worst handwriting. Surely we always did our best.

I never had to look for anything, I simply read out things on the list and the clever grocer went to the appropriate shelf with an air of knowledge that just had to be admired. It was an ancient term known as the personal touch. There were no giant superstores that sold everything back then. Even buying candles for a pending power cut meant going to the local hardware shop that stank of paraffin. That particular shop sold nails, pointless lengths of chain and electrical things that were never on a shopping list given to me by my mother. Grocer's shops sold groceries, butcher's shops sold butchered meat and it seemed to me that hardware shops sold things that were hard to wear. That was my childhood logic and I still marvel at its innocence.

It would all change with the arrival of the supermarket, when many small shopping lists became one big strip of items and little kids like me didn't have the strength to carry the goods home or carry enough money in our trousers to pay such a large bill. That was the other thing that has changed so much, everything was paid for in cash. There were no credit cards until Barclaycard came up with the bright idea in 1966, quite possibly to celebrate England winning The World Cup. Just think, if Geoff Hurst had never scored that hat-trick there would be no such thing as a credit card. Mum trusted me with a couple of five-pound notes, but I hasten to add she never trusted me with her cheque book. Cash was king.

There were ten-shilling notes too, or ten bob notes as we affectionately called them, the equivalent of 50 pence in today's money. They were a kind of reddish-brown tint and they represented a minor form of wealth. Imagine if 50ps were made of paper today, we would have stripped the forests of the world bare and numerous animals would have become extinct. It confirms the fact that money doesn't grow on trees, or as trees to be gramatically correct. I now pause as I check the spelling of that long word. Best I sling in another letter m. Grammatically.

The shops grew bigger as I grew bigger and the days of shopping around disappeared into oblivion, leaving me with just the memories of how I ran the errands for my parents.

More memories come flooding back to me right now as I recall how I finely tuned the art of food shopping. I did it every Saturday for many years, a seasoned campaigner I became. It only took an hour and a half and I never had to stop off for a coffee and a chat with a fellow shopper. I just got on with it, fully focussed, until the job was done and the change was safely in my piggy-bank.

It would only be right here to emphasise my hatred of screaming kids running loose in modern day supermarkets. I was never a screaming kid, I had manners. I only ever screamed when a spider landed on me and that had to be a fairly big one, or if my brother thumped me with his bicycle pump. The big stores are places where babies now scream louder and longer than anywhere else and spoilt brats sulk until they are allowed a bar of chocolate to shove in their annoying mouths. Babies do enough screaming in the maternity hospitals when they first stick their heads out. I understand that, but you'd think they would have calmed down a bit by the time they get to being pushed around in prams. No chance. Sometimes, there's just no pleasing screaming babies is there? Whatever happened to the good old dummy in the mouth and rocking backwards and forwards in the push-chair? You seldom hear parents singing rock a bye baby on the tree-top in a supermarket. They're usually far too busy chatting on their mobiles. Such baby noise is something I haven't been missing in the slightest since I recently locked myself indoors, followed by a confinement to barracks, forced upon me by those in Westminster. We all have to admit how much we adore other people's children, knowing deep down most of them are annoying little creatures. Yes, we still have to gaze at endless photos on our phones and on social media, but the lack of screaming every time we go shopping has become a small mercy at this time. I remember someone once telling me they loved kids but they couldn't eat a whole one.

Young ones driving supermarket trolleys around are a menace too and it has been a delight to see the demise of such useless drivers, far too young to have passed any kind of driving test, in control of such four-wheeled vehicles. They cause untold havoc with their lack of aisle-sense, a fact proven by the number of supermarket trolleys found in rivers and car parks, with no kids attached I should point out, a fact that may go to prove that children are taught to swim far too young these days. Kids are the road-ragers of tomorrow, make no mistake, and that's something the supermarkets must shoulder the blame for.

You may recall they even brought in the idea of having to insert a pound coin to get hold of such a vehicle in the hope kids would keep their grubby hands off and wouldn't waste their pocket money on such an investment, but it didn't really work. Paying a pound for the privilege of buying food? Don't start me off on that one. The very honour of paying to walk into a shop to hand our money over to a cashier. I never thought the public would tolerate that for one minute, but my doubts were unfounded. It's true you get your money back when you return the trolley to its rightful place but that makes it more unbelievable it needs to be inserted in the first place. The claim is that it stops them being stolen. I have visited many friends during the time I was allowed to and I never saw a stolen supermarket trolley in their living-rooms or bathrooms.

Let's not even go near the idea of having to pay for bags in a supermarket. Isn't it annoying when a cashier looks at your seventeen items and asks if you need a bag? I so feel like them telling them I will be fine as I have a pet octopus in the car who will pop in and gather them up as soon as I have paid. Is it really a means of helping the environment? If there were no bags around how would kind, thoughtful people collect the discarded rubbish from our beaches? I know what you're thinking, but I haven't spoken to anyone for three months and I think it is beginning to tell at a time when people like us are considered to be unwanted rubbish ourselves. The scatter-gun brain is at work again.

As I write, I realise how much I hate the arrogance and din of supermarkets and I think the world has become, despite the added difficulties, a far more placid place since their part-closure and new methods of selling have come to be. Their few months out of the usual action have been a joy to behold to me, albeit for such a short period. It's all such a far cry from taking mum's shopping list and bringing home her instructions in a carrier bag. Online shopping with an App? Waiting in a queue longer than any seen outside a football stadium or cinema? Greedy buggers stealing pasta from other trolleys? Shelf-stackers asking my age? Stop the world, I want to get off.

That damn song of fifty years ago has become an earworm that just will not go away.

Grocer Jack, grocer Jack, get off your back, go into town, don't let them down, oh no, no.

Chapter Four – The Butcher's Shop

Brace yourself because a visit to the old traditional butcher's shop was not an experience for the faint hearted. Their displays were hardly modelled on subtlety and it didn't help matters when they stood behind the counter proudly sporting their bloodstained aprons, clutching sharpened knives ready for action.

Butchers were always big, stocky men who, without a shadow of a doubt, looked like butchers and not ballet-dancers. The only down-side was they all wore stupid straw hats as if they were about to take part in some corny American musical. They all seemed muscle bound too, capable of strangling a buffalo with one hand while breaking a coconut in half with the other. You never saw an underweight butcher who weighed six stone soaking wet, standing behind the counter wielding a bloodstained axe, and for that very reason butchers weren't people to pick an argument with, in any kind of safety at least. It's true they all had a young apprentice who was covered in adolescent spots who seemed to stand around holding a broom, but the butcher himself was a stocky chap who enjoyed the more macabre side of life. Would you argue with a man holding a sharp knife? Exactly. I considered it once, but I thought better of it, not wishing to mar my appearance and all I was trying to do was watch a football match.

I seem to remember that most people ate meat when I was young. Vegetarians hadn't really been allowed into the country and nor had they admitted to their worthy cause, so meat-eating was set by a timetable that few families ignored. Roasts on Sunday, cold meat leftovers the following day and then a combination of sausages, pies and mince through the week, with one day a week allotted to a piece of fish.

Butchers came in two varieties, those who woke up at dawn to attend the wholesale meat market, and those who prepared their own meat, enough said.

It wasn't unusual to see a poor rabbit hanging upside-down in the shop window like some poster for Watership Down, alongside parts of bigger animals on display. They knew what to stock due to the habit of the families of the time.

People ate pigeons too, not a great way of thanking them for their war efforts as messengers behind enemy lines. Woodpeckers and starlings did absolutely nothing in the war, yet they didn't end up in pies. My parents' generation showed little gratitude or loyalty towards their fellow war heroes.

There was a time when our ancestors even considered having a nice parrot for dinner until they passed on the idea for fear of the things repeating on them.

Pheasant and grouse were only sold in posh places, certainly not where I was brought up. I didn't have a clue what a grouse looked like until I bought a bottle of whiskey and saw it on the label. Come to think of it, I didn't know what The Houses of Parliament looked like either until I saw a picture of the place on a bottle of brown sauce that accompanied anything my dad ate. As a third and final example, I never knew what a partridge looked like either because there were no pear trees growing near to where I lived.

Sunday roasts were as part of the sacred day as going to church, if you got out of bed in time, or having a pint at lunchtime down the local pub. Roast beef with horseradish sauce sat at the top of the popularity league table, even though it boasted to be the most expensive by far, followed by lamb with mint sauce and pork with apple sauce. Nobody dared to mix up those sauces and serve beef with apple, perish the thought.

I once thought about making my own horseradish sauce to accompany my beef dinners, but I had no idea how many radishes needed to be added to what size piece of a horse and so I never bothered.

Strange as it may seem, chicken rarely featured on the Sunday lunch table. It took a few more years for chicken to soar above all others on the popularity list. Even as they became the nation's favourite, no butcher sold chicken pieces. You bought a chicken or you didn't. They were folded up and ready to place into the oven. Someone once said that if there were no wedding receptions or curry houses then the world would have been over-run with chickens. They were probably right.

All-year-round turkey? No such thing. Turkeys only came a cropper at Christmas, changing the window displays of butchers' shops around the nation. All other sacrifices were moved to the back shelves as turkeys adorned the shop windows, hanging upside-down yet fully feathered, a consideration never granted to coy, embarrassed chickens. For those seven days leading up to the festive celebration everything seemed to change. The butcher was suddenly selling packets of Paxo sage and onion stuffing and sausage meat had appeared without skins and ten times bigger than sausages. Those little pigs in blankets things hadn't even gone to market all those years ago. Bacon was only eaten at breakfast time, in a sandwich, or fried to a gum-splitting crispy state to accompany liver, but never as part of a Christmas dinner.

My mother always bought a chunk of ham too at Christmas. We never ate ham any other time of the year and she only bought it so as not to waste the jar of piccalilli that we also never ate until Boxing Day. Ham slotted, quite snobbishly I thought, into the cold meat category and we already had cold beef or lamb leftovers so there wasn't any need to add ham to our mashed-potato companions.

Don't you dare start me off on cranberry sauce. I'd never seen a wild cranberry in my life and I still haven't. I wouldn't know where to look for a cranberry tree. Why does it taste good and compliment a turkey but no other bird three-hundred and sixty-four days of the year? Christmas didn't just bring presents and hangovers, it allowed us all to experience foodstuff that, just like Father Christmas, came but once a year. Puddings with coins thrown in to cut your mouth, parsnips and an insipid coloured gravy that didn't really make the grade.

As December came around mince took up a totally different meaning. It no longer meant left-over meat that had been shoved through a mincing machine as suddenly, under a different recipe and I don't dispute that, it became something you put in pies for those who weren't too struck on Christmas pudding. If there had never been mince pies then there wouldn't have been cockney rhyming-slang and there would have been no Chas and Dave. Such a traditional thing was Christmas. Everything about it is still soaked in nostalgia and fond memories. Speaking of novelty songs and Chas and Dave, have you noticed there have been no new Christmas songs on the radio for donkey's years? Perhaps there are no new lyrics that depict Christmases of the past. Perhaps there are, you just never know.

Mince pies, Morecambe and Wise, going to sleep without closing your eyes.
Giving a card to someone at school, not getting one back and feeling a fool.
Being a shepherd in the school play, bubble and squeak on Boxing day.
Eating a layer of Cadbury's milk tray and spitting the coffee cream out.

Silent Night, Turkish delight, figs that only our grannies would bite.

A Christmas cracker's terrible joke, dad's cigars and the smell of the smoke.

Trying to remember what made you ill, not the uneaten dates on the window-sill,

blaming it all on a rotten brazil as you measured a spoonful of Andrews.

Jumping bean, a tangerine, a Pifco torch that you never turned green.

Tiddlywinking into a cup, Steve McQueen smashing his motorbike up.

When The Queen spoke to us all, there wasn't a single card on her wall

I couldn't believe she had no friends at all, and why wasn't she out in the kitchen?

Paper chains and the taste of the gum,

taking them home from school to your mum

Paper chains were never big hits, before we got home they had fallen to bits.

Unfinished jigsaws, Monopoly as well, we fell asleep before we bought a hotel.

Who did it in Cluedo no-one could tell, so we blamed The Reverend Green.

Eating Christmas pud wasn't fun when you bit on a sixpence and severed your gum.

Dad in slippers that still bore the price as he wore his new jumper and stank of old spice.

Paper hats we had to put on, but they'd ripped by the time the turkey had gone.

Though nan always managed to keep her one on as she
sipped her way through a snowball.
These are the things we remember
from the 25th December.
Memories that come back every year
Things long gone but they all reappear
When Santa Claus and his reindeer drew
They're the toast of Christmas past.

During my enforced isolation I had to ask myself
if I could do without sausages. I asked myself other
things too, but sausages were high up the list. It was a
tough call, even though we all know their contents are
somewhat dubious. Yes, they're still a major part of a
traditional English breakfast, good friends with the
bacon, but I'm not so sure they were so delicately filled
years ago, so I'm talking of the old-fashioned sausage as
opposed to its modern-day counterparts that adorn
barbecue grills in all their burnt splendour. I decided
they were an important thing to put in the freezer
whilst I stayed indoors and I still have a few packs
awaiting consumption as I write.

I don't remember the year I experienced my first
barbecue, but I definitely wasn't a child. I didn't even
attend a barbecue at college. Come to think of it, I
didn't attend most of my lessons at college either so
that's no big deal. I spent most of my time coming to
terms with home-made wine and real-ale that, judging
by its strength, was far more real than expected.
Barbecues used to be the pastime for beach-bumming

Australians until it caught on in Britain, minus the perfect weather. There can be nothing better to think about right now than sitting in the garden tackling burnt offerings as quickly as possible before the heavens open and everyone runs for cover and the grill sends caustic smoke-signals to the neighbours. I wouldn't that in the slightest. Australians were clever folk who could surf and cook a barbecue at the same time, whilst Brits like me struggled to cook a sausage alongside a burger with a stark inability to have them both ready to eat at the same time. It would be wonderful departure to at least be attempting such a calamity as I sit staring at empty garden that used to welcome so many friends to its borders. Even an empty crisp packet blowing in the breeze would somewhat of a revelation. I still cannot cook a skewer laden with meat chunks, mushrooms and tomatoes without burning the items to a cinder, yet I wouldn't mind any of that this afternoon. By way of a change I'd eat any shrivelled object so long as it is something different to the norm.

I was about to say that sausages come in all shapes and sizes, but they obviously don't as they're all long and thin. Only their length and thickness vary. It's widely stated that the things originated in Argentina of all places, the answer to which is who cares? I for one couldn't give a monkey's armpit, but it begs the question, if they originated in Argentina then why do we never sling a tin of corned beef on the grill alongside them like they obviously do? Hey, let's not get too deep here. Whatever goes in sausages is debateable and best left unsaid, but I was always curious as to where the skins came from and how the butcher loaded them into the sausage-making machine. All I can say is I wish I hadn't been so curious. In the old days, when people were far more barbaric than they are today, the skins were made from cleaned animal intestines, but times have fortunately changed and most are now produced from such materials as collagen and cellulose. So, thankfully, some sausages are made with plastic skins.

Ok, we move on from the dubious sausages, but what the hell was offal, apart from the fact it sounded like something awful? Luckily my parents hated offal which meant it was never included in my food shop, yet I remember staring at the stuff on many occasions, wondering who on earth would dare to eat such a pile of unsavoury animal sediment. It looked like white gloss paint when the lid had been left off the tin for a fortnight. I personally cannot subscribe to its addition to anyone's diet but, by all accounts, it is highly nutritious and contains vitamins and minerals vital to our own well-being. Even so guys! In a nutshell, even though offal isn't a nut and it doesn't come in shells, it's anything within an animal's body that isn't muscular. I suppose that's the nicest way of putting it and our ancestors ate it by the shovel-load. No thanks. If offal made our grandparents, and even further back, more healthy, then why did most of them die before they reached their late fifties? If offal proved to be answer of longer life, packing us full of vitamins, I'm glad I was a spotty, skinny kid with a skin complaint who girls turned their backs on. Give me a nice juicy apple any day. It seemed to keep the doctor away as boasted. Having said that, my own grannie suffered a failed kidney and an apple didn't do her any good whatsoever. Neither did the doctor as she died a few months later, even though she'd probably made numerous trips to the butcher shop in her lifetime to collect her dollops of offal to keep her going.

Another thing I never quite understood about the butcher's shop was the vast quantities of sawdust sprinkled on the shop floor. Surely it meant something unsavoury and quite unmentionable? Yes, every butcher's shop had black and white tiled flooring with sawdust rising in piles like sand-dunes on a beach. Did they really need to do that? Was the shop floor really covered in the dreaded red stuff that needed to be soaked up under foot? I cannot think of any other reason as to why they would have bothered. I know my mum would never allow me to wear my best shoes on the rare occasion I went there.

All this talk about the butcher's shop, but the food shop expedition I undertook, on behalf of my mum and dad, rarely took me to such an establishment I'm pleased to say, and as I think back it may well have been a decision made for me by my mother who probably didn't want me to witness the result of some animalistic battlefield or send me somewhere that caused her to buy me a new pair of shoes. I don't know who bought the meat for our family, but it certainly wasn't me. I was king of the groceries. Maybe she assigned my older brother who would have done it with not so much as a single stomach churn. There were certainly unpleasantries associated with the place that young eyes should not have observed.

After the war, people of my parents' generation considered tongue a bit of a delicacy. It was always the tongue of an ox due to the size of the beast. A lamb's tongue would hardly have filled any stomach. I have sympathy for the poor ox. Our ancestors made soup from its tail and then got stuck into its tail. When you think about it the poor beast could have continued living if it hadn't have minded not speaking much or having its rear end covered in flies due to the lack of swishing. I would have imagined eating a tongue sandwich to be a real risk anyway as the brain tried to work out which tongue was which inside one's mouth. We all went through the childhood phase of biting our own tongues, so the whole idea seemed far too dangerous to even contemplate. Luckily, I never had to.

I also have to admit to enjoying the taste of liver far more than I ever did looking at it. It always reminded me of a jellyfish that had gone rusty. With crispy bacon and mashed potato it constituted a regular meal in our household, usually on a Wednesday night in winter.

As I have grown older, something we all seem to go through, I still seem to give those kind of shops a wide berth. Of course, there is no logic in such hypocritical madness. I eat meat, I enjoy meat, but I prefer to buy it packed nicely, all safe and sound in little trays and covered with that plastic stuff that perhaps they also use now for making the casings of sausages. I have no idea. Despite my obvious passion for nostalgia I have no desire to return to the days when the poor victims hung from the gallows like trophies. Lambs leap up and down in fields and chickens run around as if they're at some kind of drug-induced, midnight rave party, I know that, so I don't need to see them in such unfortunate poses of defeat, particular as I seem to feel in a similar mood at present. This is probably the closest I have ever come to becoming a vegetarian as I share their sense of hopelessness and pain.

Before being banned from shopping by the government I often patrolled and scanned the meat aisle of my local supermarket, admiring the many shades of pink on display. It all seemed so different to the traditional butcher's shop, hardly surprising as most meats are now prepared and sold as additions to the freezer and seldom eaten fresh, especially at this particular time. There certainly weren't sprinkling of sawdust down the aisle.

My mother and father didn't have a freezer. God no, Mrs Davey, next door, was the first woman in our street to own a fridge, let alone a freezer. It was called an Electrolux and was a size no bigger than a microwave oven. Such an acquisition made her the poshest person in our street, possibly for miles. It had an ice-cube section and I loved going round to see her for my first ever cold orange squashes. Oh, how she loved to boast that her milk lasted three days longer than anyone else's before it came out in nasty lumps as though it had caught something contagious from the butter. I wasn't quite sure what she was talking about, but we won't go there as I never remember her being pregnant in the first place.

Did you know the first domestic fridge did not appear in Britain until 1947, two years after the war ended? More to the point, do you really care? Who would? I wonder where our grandparents used to keep the piles of offal.

As far as my parents were concerned, I've moved off my grandparents, the fridge was nothing more than a luxury item they couldn't really afford if dad was going to continue smoking and drinking copious pints of beer down the pub. They were the kind of luxuries he preferred and we had to go along with his preferences as he was our family breadwinner. Mum used to buy wool to knit jumpers, another total financial indulgence that kept a sparkling new fridge at bay, so she didn't really help matters. If dad had given up smoking our family may well have afforded a holiday every year too, but dad wouldn't lay on a beach for fear of skin cancer, so he smoked instead and kept himself healthy that way. Clever man was my dad, not one to have wool pulled over his eyes, especially when dear mum was knitting.

I remember a time when he brought our cat home from the vet and hung him from the ceiling, telling us the lampshade around the poor animal's neck looked much better than the one in our living-room. Oh yes, a clever man alright. I shudder to think who my father would blame for the dreadful current state of affairs. He would never have blamed Great Britain or the Great British people.

So, food shopping for freezer items, getting back to the point, didn't exist when I undertook my first food shopping expeditions and yet it's hard to imagine shopping now without buying things that would stock up the freezer. All of a sudden, it's all that matters, far more than fresh food that will be gone or perhaps gone off in a couple of days.

The way the recent dreaded year has transpired it has become a valuable white good in the kitchen that prevents us from dying of starvation, a fact that made me wonder if, in which case, our parents, mine in particular, and my grandparents, all died of starvation themselves and not of other ailments of the time. Maybe the death certificates were nothing more than fiction, not that it matters to them anymore.

So, there you have it, dear reader. The across-the-board food shop upon which I gained my own experience of such a deed was a splintered affair that never took place in just the one shop like it does in modern times. It also didn't include me buying meat for the reasons mentioned. All the items, enough to see my family through the week, fitted into just two carrier bags or I would never have managed to have walked them home, one in each hand. Having said that, the Saturday morning food shop didn't include vegetables. Their purchases were excluded until later in the day, all part of the food shop ritual, a remarkably shrewd relevance of which will become clear.

During my youth, every Saturday had been mapped out for me. All shops opened at 8 o'clock, none of this 24-hour, open all day nonsense that had only been invented for insomniacs and burglars who wanted to buy a few bits and pieces on their way home from work. I did the food shop, the grocery section, first thing, before going off to play football for my school. I would come home, scrape the mud off my knee-caps, clean the brass, cook my dad sausages and chips and, later in the afternoon, the second retail assault would take place when I visited the greengrocer, Mr Balding. He closed at 6pm prompt and I never went in there until half an hour before the shutters came down.

For some very strange reason Mr Balding looked like the kind of bloke who ran a garden centre, mainly because he always wore a beige cardigan with leather patches on the elbows and his hair sprouted out like a cauliflower. All his relatively fresh goods were in boxes outside the front of the shop. There were relatively piles of fresh fruit, relatively new potatoes and relatively strong onions, all sitting next to each other, in neat lines on strips of pretend grass. Beside them, by the door, stood Mr Balding, greeting passers-by with a welcoming wave and a smile that revealed a gap in the middle of his stained teeth. I still see those tasty goods now and realise what was missing, the things didn't exist in a shop back then. No butternut squash or avocados, more like rhubarb and swede.

He often gave babies an apple to chew on, just the one bite with tender gums until a disrespectful mother would sling it on the pavement two shops down. I once told him my sister had been rushed to hospital and he set about selecting and bagging-up a bunch of grapes until she appeared behind me looking bemused. It was worth a try. He clipped me round the ear, that's what adults did back then to naughty boys like me without fear of arrest, getting their names in the local paper or being added to the child abuse register. We all hit each other back then, sometimes for no reason at all. Kids hit kids in the playground, teachers caned kids in the classroom, coppers on bikes hit kids for scrumping apples and parents hit their children for more reasons than I care to remember. My dad's stupid words still ring loud and clear in my ears;

'Get me something to hit you with.' I would go and find him a balloon.

The late-afternoon vegetable shop had method in its madness, I should make that clear, and it happened as regular as clockwork. As soon as I'd heard the football results on the radio I was on my way, arm muscles flexed and ready for heavy lifting. Football injuries permitting, I ran as fast as I could, tennis ball in my hand, pretending to be one of my favourite professional footballers who had scored that afternoon. Mr Balding liked children and always greeted me with a smile, unlike the nasty, scary-looking butcher. He seemed to smell of spinach, but that may well have been the goods that were scattered around him, if not a most undesirable after-shave lotion.

I feel the vegetable shop is worthy of deeper description.

Chapter Five – The Vegetable Shop

I always enjoyed the vegetable shop, or greengrocers, call it what you will. I suppose it was the nearest I ever came to visiting the countryside, what with its beautiful colours and smells. There was an equally beautiful and young Saturday girl working there who I found far more attractive than the parsnips and with far whiter teeth than Mr Balding's set. I remember wondering if she went to my school before realising I went to a boys' school so the chances were remote, as were my chances of ever asking her out, let alone marry her. Whatever the odds stacked against me, yes she was far fitter than a fully grown parsnip. Hang on, I now recall she had ginger hair, curled with the fury of youth, so it would be far more accurate to say she looked far more attractive than a mature carrot. Error amended on my read through.

The vegetable food shop took place just before they closed for the weekend, so they had to get rid of their stock before it went limp on the Sunday when they were closed. It was the perfect time to reap some bargains and my astute mother knew that only too well when she made me go there so late in the day.

I shudder to think how much food wastage has occurred through the shopping ban of recent times. I knew milk had been dumped down the drain by farmers, such a savage crime. It must have been the same for any shop that sold fresh items such as greengrocers, bakers, florists and garden centres. It isn't any wonder the world is heading for an economic slump of massive proportions. Mr Balding let nothing go to waste, selling everything off at a ridiculously low price as he stored the empty boxes off the street and back into the shop. Any un-sold fruit and veg he left outside on the street, a kind gesture to the dishonest members of our neighbourhood who needed strength and energy to maintain their criminal activities. Strangely, possibly not so strangely, Mr Balding's shop was never burgled or vandalised, a kind of mutual respect thing I suppose.

First on mum's list were five pounds of potatoes, not in plastic bags back then, but loose. They were weighed on scales and tipped into your shopping bag along with various lumps of mud and insects, so they had to go in first or they would have flattened the other purchases, especially the tomatoes. We loved potatoes in our house. We hero-worshipped all the different varieties from roast to boiled, from new to mash, and, of course, chips. I would never have envisaged frozen chips sold in bags that you could keep in the freezer before heating them up in the oven. That was nothing more than a ridiculous idea that would never happen. It was about as unlikely as pre-prepared, frozen, shop-bought Yorkshire puddings and onion rings. Impossible, as ridiculous as frozen shepherds pie and bubble and squeak. When freezers first found their place in the kitchen kids were fed fish-fingers in colossal numbers. New owners didn't really know what to put in them. Fish-fingers, steak and kidney pies, fish fingers and endless packets of peas. There wasn't room for international cuisine exploration.

I knew what I was doing, I placed half the potatoes in the bottom of one bag and the other half in the other, thus keeping a sense of equilibrium. Yeah, I'd done it before. Next came two pounds of peas. There was always something satisfying about sitting in the living-room shelling peas on a Sunday morning, in preparation for the Sunday lunch. The taste of raw peas still lingers in my memory. Mum would make me place all the shells into a bag so she could boil them up and make pea-soup, which, strangely enough, we didn't just have on winter days when we were shrouded in thick fog. Nothing was ever wasted, apart from dad when he came home from the pub on a Saturday night.

I used to love preparing the vegetables, it seemed quite a grown-up thing to do, what with the handling of a sharp knife, the kind of which seem to be carried around these days by many kids over thirteen years of age as a kind of fashion statement. We never stabbed each other when I was at school, not even in a friendly way. We swapped bubble-gum cards and played football together. If there happened to be a kid in class we didn't like we used to let off a stink-bomb under his seat and laugh as the teacher sent him outside for being so inconsiderate to others. Stabbing became a bragging trip for grown-ups who joined gangs and couldn't think of anything better to do. The nearest I came to being stabbed was when I joined the boy scouts and I tripped over with a penknife in my pocket that had been given to me by my brother for my birthday. If the penknife had been open I may well have bled to death after colliding with a badly laid paving slab. Suing the council? I don't think so. A quick plaster job and then back to getting on with my life. I'd never heard of anyone suing the council, it didn't enter anyone's head. It's a shame I was of such tender years because I would loved to have sued them. They put mum and dad's rent up and the dustmen emptied rubbish in the hallway of our council flats because we couldn't afford to leave a Christmas tip. A tip for non-tip you could say if you're not too bothered about you grammar.

Then there were the runner beans. They weren't my favourite vegetable by any means as they seemed to be held together by string thick enough to wrap a parcel. They became a green, tangled mass in your mouth which you had to swallow in one go to reap the goodness of the things. And why were they called runner beans anyway? They never ran anywhere, preferring to lay limply, side by side, with black edges, like British holidaymakers before airlines went bust and Spanish holidays were placed on hold.

Into the shopping bag then went carrots, greens, a solitary cauliflower that fed five of us, and occasionally broad beans that, once again, I wouldn't describe as particularly broad, more rotund. That was about it as far as I remember. Both bags were three-quarters full as I completed the vegetable shop with fruit. We only ever ate apples and oranges, plus tangerines at Christmas. The first bananas hadn't arrived in Britain during my early days and grapes were only for people dying in hospital, so long as they shared them with the visitors as they lay there gasping for breath. There wasn't any need to be inconsiderate just because were having a tough time.

I try to relate all the above to my last legal visit to a supermarket a short time ago, not including the final desperation shop that followed. It had become a different world. I felt so spoilt for choice as I slowly pushed my trolley along long lines of fresh stuff. Peppers? Green ones, orange ones and red ones, I only ever saw those colours at a set of traffic lights, never on my dinner plate. Aubergines? Broccoli? Where the hell did they come from and when did they first appear as part of our stable diets? Why were they all such awkward spellings? There was over twenty yards of different potatoes, different sized onions from various countries and enough tomatoes to fend off the greenhouse effect. Masses of cucumbers lay suffocating on top of each other and spring onions looked as if they were strangled by elastic bands.

Corn on the cob was another luxury I missed out on as a child. For the life of me I don't know if the bright yellow things were around as I grew up, but if they were we never had them because both my parents had false teeth and there wasn't anything worse for them than trying to bite into an undercooked corn on the cob. My dad would have taken one bite and slung it across the room as though it were a hand-grenade in the trenches. Not content with a violent act, it would be followed by yet another story of how he liberated France and how they didn't deserve it because the common decency to speak English. Corn on the cob was nothing more than a stick of dynamite ready to have its fuse lit every time dad tried to defend The British Empire.

It's been a few months now since I passed all those new-fangled vegetables in the supermarket before parking my trolley at the salad stuff, never thinking for one moment it would be one of my final joys of retail freedom. Before the attack upon us I spent joyful hours filling a whole trolley with just salad stuff, such was my choice, but not anymore. We can't break shopping ranks now and return to grab something we'd forgotten first time around. It can only be matter of time before anyone caught committing such a crime will be sent packing to Australia for penal servitude, a long arduous trip in a sailing ship if the planes are still grounded, a scary prospect for those who don't think too much of cricket or kangaroos.

The salad shop I undertook for my parents consisted of just half a dozen tomatoes in a brown bag and a cucumber, an unsealed cucumber at that. My schoolboy salad dinners were as above with sliced onion and a few outer-leaves of a cabbage thrown in for good measure. French dressing was some bloke, riding a bike, with a droopy moustache, beret on his head and a string of onions slung around his shoulders. As for coleslaw, the nearest I ever got to coleslaw was having one of those horrible lumps coming up on my lip. As far as I recall we had a sort of half-salad of tomato and cucumber with a tin of salmon on Sunday evenings and a full salad with the other two ingredients on Boxing Day with bubble and squeak, cold turkey and pickled onions. The rest of the year we ate proper food, not the salad stuff they feed to rabbits. My dad wouldn't entertain that kind of food, preferring wholesome chunks of anything that wasn't salad.

On my final shop before lockdown, one that happened just a short time after the one I have mentioned above, I more or less ignored the vegetables and salads and concentrated on items, tinned items, that would last longer. I wasn't too bothered about pasta and I had a few toilet rolls in the kitchen cupboard, so I wasn't too bothered about that either, preferring to stay away from that particular battlefield. The nasty, selfish hoarders could have as much of that as they wanted as far as I was concerned. For some really odd reason the shop had decided to come up with some of their own illogical legislation that only allowed you to buy two of any item, so I passed on the peas and the grapes. I shot the bossy lady's plan down in flames when I asked for two cigarettes, a Benson and a Hedge. I crowded two tins of various items into my trolley.

Two tins of . . . creamed rice, various soups ranging through the obvious flavours from mushroom to vegetable as I argued that each flavour counted as two individual items, tuna fish, peeled tomatoes, butter beans, evaporated milk, baked beans, corned beef and a couple of tins of macaroni cheese that, I must admit, tasted so disgusting that the blackbirds in the garden passed after I had. That final list of non-perishables, in the belief and hope that I too would be non-perishable, couldn't have been more predictable or boring, but I sensed I would be in for the long haul, so I knew I had to do something about it.

I also spent a while at the aisle that sold medicines and toiletries. The tube of toothpaste had been rolled up as far as it would go and my enforced beard began to drag along the floor. Many of the shelves that once sported hand lotion, wipes and toilet rolls were empty, but there were still enough interesting hygiene-related items on show to help me through the months ahead.

It had all become so much easier than walking into the old-fashioned chemist shop with a prescription written in Latin and walking out with a bundle of sugar tablets that sorted out any ailment less dangerous than a heart-attack. The big supermarkets sell medicinal solutions for things I didn't even know existed. None of it bore any resemblance to Mr Jones's chemist shop. Jones was a qualified pharmacist and so there was every chance he went to college, a relatively unheard of step where I lived my early life.

You couldn't mistake the ancient chemist shop for any other retail outlet because it had massive bottles, and I mean massive, in the shop window, containing amazing coloured liquids that certainly weren't pineapple or orange juice, more likely copper sulphate juice. I still have no idea of their relevance, but they all stood in a long line in the shop window like soldiers setting off to a fancy-dress party. All the big bottles had Latin names written on them, a pointless adornment as most of the kids around my area struggled to read English, let alone Latin.

Yes, it all came flooding back to me as I walked down the supermarket aisle that offered tablets for all sorts of complaints. As I say, I never knew people could be so ill with so many dodgy things that required so many medications until I looked at what was on offer down that particular aisle.

I realised, despite my age, I am far healthier than I thought. I have my own teeth, minus three, my eyes seem to be functioning ok and I don't need the hundreds of vitamin supplement variations on offer. Bearing in mind I'm as old as a classic car I feel as though the engine is running ok, even if the chassis could do with some bodywork attention. I don't have athlete's foot, probably because I can't be bothered to run anywhere these days, and I don't need to suck things for chesty coughs. Yeah, I'm ok and definitely fit enough to take a stroll down memory lane and describe to you how the chemist shop at the chemist shop, pardon the bad English, was different to other shopping trips I was sent on as a young child. I pondered on the differences as I reached the end of that particular supermarket aisle. I'd forgotten to replenish my stock of razor blades, but there was no way I would turn round and be shouted at by a kid who'd just left school yet had been trusted with live ammunition. I'd go without, thank you very much.

When I returned home from that penultimate expedition I filled the cupboard, made myself a cup of tea and enjoyed some respite before setting off on my second phase of the very final food shop. I realised I'd added nothing to my freezer that still had plenty of room inside. My local supermarket boasted twenty-four shopping and so, under the cover of darkness, I drove off wearing sunglasses and a baseball cap. I have no idea why I felt so guilty about round two of my shop, but I did.

I parked discreetly in the corner of the car-park and made my way to the entrance with the help of the torch on my mobile phone. I assumed the store would be empty so late at night, but oh how wrong could I be. The car-park was jammed solid, I wasn't the only one who'd come up with the bright idea of sharing such hours with owls and burglars. Even Polish car-washers were going about their work in the darkness, realising it may well have been their last chance to make a few more quid. The whole scenario seemed hideous. Alfred Hitchcock sprung to mind. I don't know why, he just did.

Inside the store I witnessed a sight to behold. Where the hell did all these masses of insomniac people come from? The noise was nothing short of deafening. There were unfit men in tracksuits and women's bodies falling out of pyjamas. There were babies snoring in prams with dummies hanging from their mouths and a security guard sound asleep by the entrance. Weary shelf-stackers were doing their very best to stack shelves, the queues were endless and the staff announcements were louder than The Rolling Stones. It all reminded me of a central city railway station on Christmas Eve as people hurried backwards and forwards with trolleys and numerous large boxes of equally large things. Surely this wasn't the time to be buying a new set of saucepans and a cheap tea service? Was it really the time to splash out on a new wide-screen television? There had to be far more important things to load up and get home?

The barbecue area was understandably deserted as we all knew such social occasions wouldn't be happening for a while. Nobody appeared too bothered about lighter fuel and stupid little lanterns you stuck in the lawn. We all knew those days were gone and wouldn't be returning for some time. Bags of kindling gathered woodworm as they awaited new owners. It just wasn't to be.

Sticking to my plan, I made my way straight to the frozen food section, as did so many other shoppers, and I waited as crowds of people gathered up all sorts of things they'd never eaten before. It seemed that if there was a sell-by date of a few months on the packet they bought it.

The second phase of my shop completed I felt ready for a couple of weeks self-isolation.

I only had one more trip to make and that could wait until the following morning. I'm sure you understand my confusion. My final shopping trip wasn't really my last trip, neither was my second trip for frozen foods my last. In all, I made three trips in two days, although I still think of it as all rolled together in a final fling before my imprisonment. That third and final excursion took me to a huge electrical goods store in the hope of purchasing a few music-related items that would help me through my boredom period. Some chance. Have you noticed, like me, that these huge stores are always out of stock of anything you want to buy?   I just don't get why they only seem to have one of everything, that one being the one on display and therefore not for sale. It could be a computer, a washing-machine, a set of headphones, even a 13 amp plug. There's just the one unless you hit lucky.

Some young lad gets on his tablet and checks. You know he's wasting your time. He knows he's wasting his own time too. He tells you they either have what you want in the Swindon branch or that he can order one in five days and it will be an extra twenty quid for delivery. It's not just me is it? How many different kinds of wide-screen televisions and computers do these places sell? Why don't they cut the numbers on display down by half and have a few spare ones out the back in the hope a customer will buy one of them?

The last, bizarre thing of all is when you order one for future delivery yet, still not in possession of your new purchase, they try their darndest to sell you a three-year warranty cover. As if, but that's how those big places make their money. They're interlinked with insurance companies who pay them a commission each time you take up the wonderful offer. It's a sly but clever business plan but only if they manage to sell you something in the first place. I wouldn't mind buying a three-year warranty on myself right now, let alone a cut-price MP3 player.

I tried to explain to the young man, best I could, that I couldn't wait five days as I headed into self-isolation that afternoon. It's incredible how disinterested he then became. I hadn't even finished my sentence before he looked me up and down, evaluated me as an ageing, complete waste of time, and walked away to offer help to a younger man who wasn't a vulnerable self-isolator, someone whose age allowed them to enter into that three-year warranty plan. No commission, no manners or professional sales skills. It was as simple as that. I don't know why, and I'm definitely well out of order, but I sense he may well have been one of the younger kids that defied orders and sat on the beach drinking beer with his mates during lockdown, when he should have been helping the nation to win the battle. Put it this way, he was an unhelpful little shit, enough said. Three-year warranty indeed. Take a hike, I'll get my new washing-machine somewhere else should this one die in the next few months. Hang on, why do I need to be washing clothes anyway? I'm not going anywhere for the foreseeable future. I'd reached a time in my life when it was more important to wash my hands with far more regularity than my clothes. Sadly, long before the nasty visitor, I happened to be attending more funerals than weddings, but even that didn't involve too much washing of clothes as it was the same suit, the same shirt, but with a different tie. I bought my first black tie fifteen years ago and it has come out the drawer more times than I had expected. Now we are going through a phase where even funerals are out of bounds. Words fail me as I have a feeling of disgust in my guts.

My final food shop, all three parts of it, for a while at least, was complete and my electrical goods shopping expedition had been a complete non-starter. On the drive home, as I tried to explain to my car that we wouldn't be meeting up for a while, I was reminded of the various complexities I encountered when shopping for my folks and how things had changed so much over the years. The current situation had swiftly sent me back to the days when I shopped without a car.

Shops always held stock and sales staff had a modicum of politeness about them. Yes, it's true that some shops were harder to be taken seriously than others when you're just a little boy with a list your mother had written out, but I always seemed to get some kind of a result. That's how I came to think about Mr Jones the chemist.

The trip to his chemist shop I still recall as the trickiest one by far, it was always going to be. A young boy meeting up with a man who could read Latin? I knew the odds were stacked against me on an intellectual level, but I still had to go there, such were the demands of my mother.

I stated at the beginning of my story that I had no idea how many words I could offer you, but I have to say I'm surprised by the many thoughts and recollections that have entered my head. It has been an amazing therapy and the thoughts keep coming. Maybe it is pertinent for me to turn my attentions to Mr Jones, at a time we I could do with a tablet or two for this over-active brain of mine. The chemist shop, now then, is a tricky one. I shall put the kettle on and take you back to the late 1950s. We'll have to walk as there are no other means of transport right now. Please excuse the defined limp and the walking stick.

Chapter Six – The Chemist Shop

You had to act like a grown-up to enter a chemist shop as a child. It was definitely a no-go area most of the time for youngsters such as myself, as the premises contained bottles and yet more bottles of nasty things such as chemicals and poisons, to say nothing of drugs and grown-up things such as contraceptives and laxative syrup. For that reason, my mother rarely sent me to the chemist shop for anything other than for one awkward exception.

Every time I went to such a mysterious shop on such a mysterious shop I took a personal note in a sealed envelope, a note written by my mother containing words that were not for young one's eyes. I recall how the chemist would read the note before looking at me over his spectacles with beady eyes. I stood before him in both ignorance and innocence as he disappeared into a back room before returning, clutching a brown paper parcel. I was instructed to run straight home and not leave the parcel anywhere where it could have been damaged or stolen. I must have encountered a feeling comparable to some terrorist about to plant an explosive. Only the contents were miles apart, chalk and cheese.

It took me a few years to work out exactly what that brown paper parcel contained and I think I am now of an age where I can confess, without acute embarrassment, they were sanitary towels for my mother. Of course they were for my mother, my dad never used them and my sister was far too young. I was young myself and didn't know their purpose anyway, so I will never understand why the letter in the sealed envelope and the shady look by the chemist had been deemed necessary. The chances of me leaving such a parcel at the foot of a goalpost in the park or at a friend's house were remote, regardless of the contents.

The only other time I ventured into the chemist shop occurred when prescriptions needed to be handed in and medicines collected. Just imagine that happening in today's mad world, an eight or nine-year-old kid strolling into a pharmacy and collecting a load of drugs and walking out with not so much as a buy your leave. Yes, I know it may well happen in various dodgy areas of inner-cities, but the kids would probably be armed or have some horrible man waiting outside to collect the contraband. Having said that, I don't think they would have been that interested in what was in my mum's parcel. They would fetch very little money on the black market, even just once a month.

Let's not forget the other obvious that also remained out of bounds to me. The one thing sold by the chemist that every man and boy considered an essential addition to their back-pocket, even if they

never used them. The shuddering moment in the
chemist shop I can best describe in rhyme;

A while ago when just a lad
I had girlfriend, name of Glad.
Gladys never laughed a lot
and if she hears this story, she'll have me shot,
but once she rang me up.

She said 'It's Gladys, want to come round?'
Her whispering tones were a welcome sound.
I put the phone down, punched the air
I ironed some jeans and washed my hair.
To get some flowers and things to wear
to the shops I duly stumbled.

Now the chemist's was first port of call
to get a packet of ….. to buy a packet of cotton wool.
No, not quite what I had in mind
but when I saw the queue behind
and with the chemist leering, most unkind,
my words became sort of jumbled.

The Chemist's shop, what can I say?
I still re-live that awful day.
My mouth went dry my legs went weak.
I saw them but I couldn't speak.
They were up there on the shelf but squeak,
the words just wouldn't come.

There they were, but I couldn't ask,
then I drummed up courage…… and bought a flask
Razor blades, shaving foam,
some Lucozade and a plastic comb.
What I needed most I left alone.
The chemist knew but wouldn't help me.

I left the chemist's shop incensed.
I'd spent ten pounds and fifteen pence.
All that cash I'd gone and spent
all because my bottle went.
That chemist, he knew what I meant,
ten pounds, fifteen pence.

I'd nothing left to get the wine
and I was quickly running out of time.
Round to Glad's I sprinted hard,
I felt more nervous with each yard.
I knocked politely, on my guard.
Her mother smiled and said.

'You must be Richard come on in.
Glad's upstairs she's in a spin.
You are all she ever talks about
Me and my husband we're going out.
You'll be wanting time alone no doubt.
Sit down I'll go and get her.'

The door creaked open in came Glad
'Richard I'd like to introduce my dad'

'Pleased to meet you son' he said.
My God I could have dropped down dead.
'We're ballroom dancing,' he then said,
'perhaps you'd like to join us?'

'Oh yes I really, really would.'
He looked and with a grunt said 'good'
'Gladys go upstairs get dressed.'
She didn't really seem impressed.
She gave me such a mouthful.

'It's not my fault,' I promised Glad.
'It all went wrong when I met your dad.
When I saw him well I could have died'
'What's wrong with him?' Glad replied.
'That's when I decided to confide.
'How long's he been a chemist?'

Although it's a poem I wrote many years ago it still
holds good and makes my feet curl today, outlining the
fear and trepidation of a chemist knowing exactly what
you're after but making your life as difficult as possible. I
lived it, I went through it once a few years later, and it
was only to be big-time because I didn't even have a
girlfriend. I remember throwing away the contents and
keeping the small box they came in, just in the hope my
friends would notice it and my parents wouldn't.
Contraceptives always came in packets of three, quite
an assumption that the rampant male would be

enjoying more than one session of horizontal refreshment.

Their nicknames changed through the years too. They started out as French letters, a title they didn't even understand over in France. They then became known as Johnnies, rubbers, Willie-wellies and cock sock. In Australia it's known as a dinger and Americans call it a love glove. All jolly good fun of course, but in more academic circles they have been, and always will be, sheaths and condoms. At my age I have no problem confessing that the last lot I bought had a sell-by date written in Roman numerals, nothing more than silicon memories in a brain that had far more important things to be thinking about.

The whole embarrassing event was eased when hairdressers, or barbers as they were known, began selling the same items to gentlemen who had spruced up their appearances for the coming weekend. It seemed only right to offer the additional accessory to those on a potential ego-trip that may well have resulted in the real thing. After all, there was no other reason to get your haircut.

One brand was called Ona, which is possibly where the term 'one careful owner' came from, and then there was Durex.

Durex started life in 1915 as a side-line product of The London Rubber Company, nowhere near as erotic, and the last rubber slid off their assembly line in 2007. They may enjoy a wonderful resurgence in the not too distant future as friends meet up again and life returns to normal because we all hope the forthcoming baby boom outstrips the number of divorce cases that will be rampaging through the courts all across the nation. Yes, I'm convinced after such a long and arduous experience for everyone there will either be a rise in pregnancies that will outstrip the post Second World War era by a country mile, or the divorce rate will fly through the roof tiles of houses that will be split into two financially. It will become fodder for comedians when they are able to get back on stage and perform once more.

'I divorced my wife and the house was divided into two. I got the outside and she got the inside. I don't like the idea of marriage. Why not just find someone you don't like and give them half of everything you own?'

I see such gags peppering audiences in the not too distant future, probably in silence as people are segregated into small sections in a theatre, regardless of political correctness. Political correctness? Let's not go into the correctness of politicians as we re-live this terrible time in the future. History will account their actions so there's no need us wasting time through these pages. We all accept things will never be the same again, but it will be interesting to watch the share price of rubber companies soar through the roof. The rise in popularity of the rubber contraceptive may well outstrip the drop in sales of car tyres as vehicles remain parked up, out of commission and neglected, due to the travel clampdown. Let's all hope our own bodies are not parked up, out of commission and neglected too.

I'm trying to work out when rubbers changed from items in a school pencil-case to things boys carried in their pockets in expectation. I don't think I knew what the new-fangled things were until I reached my teens as we never had sex lessons at school. No, we never stretched the things onto cucumbers as we watched the girls go red. The brown parcel and the packet of three remained mysteries to me for more years than perhaps they should have, but hey, I was far too busy playing football anyway to meet up in the park with a willing sexual participant. Now I am old I must no longer think about meeting someone in a park for such a reason as it would end up with a stiff prison sentence, if you'll pardon the pun.

Talking of days gone by is all very well, but I'm well aware the hairdressers is closed until further notice, forcing us all to get our scissors out of the drawer and end up looking like unkempt scarecrows. A kind of pride has developed on social media as sad people show off their pathetic attempts to the world outside. The entire nation seems to have been dragged through a hedge backwards and we're laughing it all off, which can't be a bad thing when smiles and laughter are in such short supply. With none of us looking at our best I think it only right we all stop worrying about condoms and our appearances and concentrate on more important things, like survival.

I will allow my memory cells to take one last look around the old-fashioned chemist shop before moving onto the supermarkets of today. It was a clutter of boxes and bottles that filled the counter and the shelves. There were bottles of cod liver oil, National Health orange juice, cherry-flavoured medicines for babies who wouldn't stop crying, boxes of tissues for my sister who wouldn't stop crying and my mum's very own favourite contraceptive, the headache tablet, something that meant my dad wouldn't stop crying.

Maybe more in keeping with today's dilemma they also sold bath cubes. Yes, every chemist had a gift section, and six bath cubes in a box constituted a gift. What exactly was a bath cube? The simple answer is it was a cube you put in the bath, there you go.

Long before bottles of bath foam, bath salts and shower gels the only way to make a bath smell nice was to sling in the regulation bath cube. As far as I know, the only exception was Cleopatra, an Egyptian woman who looked remarkably like Elizabeth Taylor, who lay in a tub of milk, assuming that was true. Imagine that, lying there, trying to relax, with an armada of cornflakes bobbing around your person like some kind of cereal regatta. Surely, porridge would blended in better. Most days I can't even be bothered to have a bath let alone take on a navel conflict with breakfast cereals.

A bath cube was built about the same size as a Lego brick and it came in two halves, a handy design within our family ranks as my mum would put one half into my water and the other half into my sister's bath after mine had been emptied. You simply threw them in and they magically dissolved down from a solid object to a powder that resembled sherbet. They came in three flavours, rose, bouquet or lavender yet they all smelt the same. It took forever to undo the wrapping and if you sat on a bath cube before it had dissolved it could be rather painful. For those two reasons alone bath cubes were a pain in the arse.

Also included in the chemist's gift section were toiletries for men and a more substantial choice of toiletries for women, it's never been any different. The men's offerings had little variation or imagination, that's never been any different either as men had little variation or imagination either, all looking the same with identical hairstyles and clothes. On display you would find Old Spice after shave lotion, Old Spice talcum powder, Old Spice shaving cream and even Old Spice soap. When the brand name began to tire they brought out Blue Strata which, if my memory serves me correctly, was Old Spice after shave lotion in a different coloured bottle. Up until that switch to Blue Strata everything came in red bottles or packets with a white sailing ship logo or cream-coloured bottles with a red sailing ship logo. The bottles were oddly shaped too, resembling a kiln at a Stoke on Trent pottery. All blokes smelt exactly the same for the best part of a decade and the air wafting around a dancehall was nothing short of unbearable. Just one kiss and girls stank of Old Spice too.

The ladies section seemed to be far more imaginative. My mum's favourite gift, her only present from me as I bought it for her every year, was either Anne French Cleansing Milk or a nice red lipstick that resembled a dog's private part. When it came to perfumes there were various cheap ranges on display such as Eau de Cologne and Eau de Toilette with long-forgotten brand names for long-forgotten friends. Chanel No 5, a classier item all round, didn't hit the shelves until 1958, when my age had almost reached double figures.

Most of the women in my schoolboy vicinity inadvertently sported the grand fragrance of Yardley because their factory was situated just down the road from where I lived, which meant many of my neighbours worked there and got the stuff half-price. They made perfume, talcum powder and hand lotion. I'm sure they made more items than that too. There were many times when my dad would say the whole area stank of Turkish brothel. At such a young age it didn't even occur to me to ask how he knew what such a place of horizontal delight stank like. Maybe he went there in the war, he may well have done as he often told the family he'd given various people a good seeing-to when posted abroad.

When it came to soap, nothing beat Cussons Imperial Leather. Every small child wondered how the badge in the middle of the tablet never wore away, causing us all to wash with far more gusto in the hope of seeing it disappear, which it never did. It was a creamy kind of soap and a welcome departure from Wright's Coal Tar or Pears.

I am at a point in my life where the smell of my body is relatively unimportant as I'm not going out anywhere for a while. I have no call for an after-shave lotion as I haven't shaved for weeks now. I would have done but my razor went blunt weeks ago. As for deodorant, well, I'm not exactly exerting myself at present, so its application is minimal. I'm not likely to be breaking into a sweat whilst watching The Antiques Roadshow with my dinner on a tray. The nearest I have come to any exercise for ages is running a bath or slicing a loaf of home-made bread. Some more energetic types have been running past my window, but not me, I'm not the type to wear lycra fabric and a headband while I keep staring at my watch. I seem to stare enough at my watch as it is these days, thank you very much. I've only ever been to a gym once, to collect my daughter and I haven't ridden a bike since I fell off on a journey home from school.

Why am I in lockdown and yet others are jogging by without masks over their mouths? I have no idea, it's all become so confusing and the conflicting daily briefs from the government haven't exactly helped. All I know is I'm over seventy and therefore my health is at threat, thus making me a burden to the medical profession who are short of staff and beds. So I just sit by the window waving at younger bodies that nonchalantly pass by. None of them ever wave back but I'm not that bothered, it being the nearest I can come to socialising at the moment. Oh, I nearly forgot, I ran to the toilet, at sprint pace, two days ago but I think that had something to do with a sell-by date in the fridge.

It's all very well limping back down memory lane with alarming regularity, possibly to the point of boredom, but I now crave for the modern-day supermarket that is so near and yet so far away.

The government seem to be encouraging two-wheeled travel as they loosen the noose and allow people to go back to work if their job cannot be fulfilled at home. There's a few problems with that one. Firstly, I can't ride a bike and, secondly, I don't have a bike, but at least the country may be moving in the right direction at last. A Medical Officer on the radio has mentioned seeing green shoots peeping their heads out of the ground. Surely she should be concentrating on her important, front-line post and not messing around in her greenhouse trying to grow tomatoes? Some people just have no sense of responsibility. On second thoughts, there are a few working in supermarkets who have maybe taken on too much responsibility.

Chapter Seven – Today's Supermarkets

I welcomed the arrival of the grand supermarket. They were opened by fading pop-stars or local Members of Parliament who nobody knew or cared about and they sold just about everything I didn't want, but they were a sign of the changing times and I longed for things to change. My parents, dad especially, had been talking about World War Two for long enough and the time had come to move on, albeit whilst pushing a trolley. At least it was something new.

Trends often move as quickly as time itself and the world we have lived in for so long will sport a different complexion in the future, that's for sure. It would have anyway, without the circumstances that occurred. The world has always been ever-changing, although not as fast as what we have experienced lately.

Even the grand word supermarket is sounding tired and jaded these days. They are now referred to as superstores by their marketing teams, another Americanism that has trespassed through the back-door of the English language. Now I am off on one, the bastardisation of our beautiful English language. Apartment is another example and an inaccurate one at that. Apartments are always joined together and yet my first flat was part of a house that contained five others, so it makes no sense at all. What about cookies? Biscuits are biscuits and I cannot in my wildest moments think of a custard cream or a rich tea as a cookie. It sounds such a childish word, totally unsuited to the grown-up dunking of a biscuit in a cup of tea, emulating our grannies. She didn't give us cookies, she gave us massive digestives that could be broken into four pieces for dunking.

I remember petrol before it became gas and sweets before they were candies. I also wore plimsolls before they became pumps. I remember asking my mum for white ones with laces instead of those black things with the piece of elastic that went over the top of my foot. They had a big, black, shiny tractor tyre on the front. Oddly enough, a supermarket, I'm sticking with that description of the place, is the only outlet that still sell the damn things. That's assuming they sell any at all as I haven't seen a young kid running around in elasticated plimsolls for over thirty years. If I saw such a sight today I would assume they were running away from their horrible parents. Kids now wear multi-coloured trainers the size of skis, with flashing lights, like a miniature version of Blackpool promenade, also on sale in the supermarket. Elasticated plimsolls? I have this image of a board-meeting and the bosses are trying to decide which line of footwear would be more exciting to a young child. Someone must have said they weren't too sure so they should stock both, just in case there was a sudden rush for the elasticated plimsoll.

Our English language had taken a turn for the worst ever since we forgave those colonials for The Boston Tea Party. I wouldn't have minded but Americans don't even drink tea, which will explain why they dumped the stuff into the sea in the first place. It didn't seem to be any great loss to them. Had my family not been such avid tea-drinkers I would never have collected cards that taught me all about wild animals, flags of the world, birds in the wild and famous ships that have long been sent to the scrapyard. Neither would I have learnt much about racing drivers and their cars, cricketers and wild flowers. Tea opened my mind back then as much as it opens my bladder today. Americans know very little about wild animals, flags and famous ships, and now you know why.

We invented the English language in the first place and, although we lent it to other nations, The United States being one, I don't see why we need to embrace such incorrect infiltrations by such incorrect infiltrators. The supermarket, or superstore, is full of so many Americanisms that it takes a while to work out what we're looking at, let alone what country we are in. Maybe we just need to take a rain-check or take five while we chill out. See what I mean? Geoffrey Chaucer never spoke like that when relating his tales from Canterbury, not a great example as I didn't understand a word he wrote either.

In recent times a shopping trolley has become a cart, crisps have become chips and chips have become French fries. An aubergine is now an eggplant. It took me long enough to familiarise myself with an aubergine, thinking at first it described a native of Australia. A courgette is now a zucchini, a lettuce has become a head of lettuce and plain chocolate is now dark chocolate. It's all part of the global language change and I, for one, happen to prefer the old names I used at the grocer's shop. Whole wheat bread used to be wholemeal bread and we covered each slice with butter or marg and not spread. Take-aways are a relatively new treat for the British and yet they have already changed their names to take-outs. Being taken away or being taken out are two entirely different things, particularly right now during this frightening time. None of these things would bother me in the slightest, I wouldn't even be thinking about them, if I wasn't hovering on the brink of depression, in need of something to whinge about.

It all made me realise why The United States has such a high suicide rate if they have to spend all their time changing all the words we gave them in the first place just to be awkward and learn new ones just to be cool. It must be so downright depressing.

We Brits knew they were going to be trouble when they decided to drive on the other side of the road, Columbus sailed in on the left hand side of the rocks and that should have been good enough for that ungrateful lot. I don't need a zip-code as I already have a postcode and it's worked fine during lockdown. I haven't had one parcel gone astray. I have a good mind to sue America for causing my depression. Perhaps I should contact my solicitor, or speak to my lawyer. In the words of Martin Luther King, a great man of words and therefore an exception to the rule, we shall overcome.

You can probably sense this has been a particularly bad day, so I'm getting an early night and will resume in the morning. Goodnight.

Phew, I needed that sleep. I'm happy to have got that one out of my system. I have woken up far more tolerant of Americans. Supermarkets are usually situated on the edge of towns and cities, away from the redundant high streets, something which obviously doesn't help the redundant high streets an inch. On the up-side, parking isn't a nightmare like it is in town centres as you never see a nasty traffic warden, or whatever those human wasps call themselves these days, something like a traffic blah blah officer I wouldn't doubt. The other benefits are cheaper prices, a place for charity fund-raisers to stand whilst freezing themselves stupid while mostly being ignored, and a few blokes with baseball-caps round the wrong way waiting to wash and wax your car like some vehicle beauty salon. The downside is obviously the demise of the good old high street as well all knew it.

It must have been around ten years ago, whilst the charity fundraisers stood around catching hyperthermia. that the high street began re-opening its doors but mainly to charity organisations. Charity shops were everywhere. Wherever you looked they were there, testing your level of generosity and awkwardness. You were a good Samaritan or you crossed the road. This all happened long before charity marathons caused chaos in our major cities. I've never seen the point of running twenty-six miles if charity begins at home. I mean to say, they can't have it both ways can they? I just thank God those runners have raised so much money for the NHS. Without those wonderful people we'd all be up shit creek without a paddle, or maybe I should say further up shit creek without a paddle, if indeed there is much further to go. How long is this creek?

Most shops or now boarded up or have been let out to more of those various charities, a good thing as charity shops will be a premium as we all try to off-load the rubbish we decided to clear from our attics, sheds and garages during lockdown. I sense, with such an overload, such shops will be more discerning than in the past, so the chances of them taking my lawnmower with a wheel missing are slim. It had to go, even though it had given good service it had started to under-perform. I had neglected its well-being for many years, never sharpening the blades so the blame was mine, but it still had to go. Just imagine having the same razor for twenty years and expecting a smooth shave. It needed to go out to stud and cut someone else's neck.

A stroll down the high street used to be such an exciting and colourful event. There were shops of all shapes and sizes, selling goods of all shapes and sizes, to customers of all shapes and sizes. Screaming kids could roam around at a distance that wasn't annoying, as opposed to a distance that has become compulsory. Buskers strummed and sang a few songs they didn't know all the way through to give the whole experience a semblance of a carnival atmosphere, something that would be most welcome at a time when all carnivals and festivals have been postponed until a much safer time.

Let's be honest, you don't get the same fun feel in a supermarket. You park your car, if it hasn't been repossessed recently for non-payment or default of the lease agreement, grab a trolley, race around as if you're on a fairground ride, pay up after you've bought a few bags that used to be free, and then you go home. The only difference is you don't go home with a coconut or a goldfish in a plastic bag.

Shopping never used to be like that. Supermarkets have squeezed the fun out of a weekend shop. Young people must be so tired of old farts such as myself going on and on and on again about the so-called good old days. They have every right to wonder if those years really were as good as they are constantly being told. I'm not too sure myself as I reflect on outbreaks of rickets, tuberculosis, three-day weeks, miners' strikes, polio and Australia retaining The Ashes. It may have been a debateable boast until this wicked infiltrator made us realise that any old day had to be a good old day compared to what we are now enduring.

So, do I miss those trips to the superstore or supermarket, whatever you choose to call the places? Not particularly. The current situation has made me realise how much I miss the small, far more friendly shops with their helpful assistants who were around before the giant sharks entered the harbour. Forgive this moment of utter indulgence as I list the high street shops I shall no longer visit. I have nothing else to do for more weeks than I care to guess and I presume you're in the same boat. They may be long gone but they are still stored in my memory bank. In my mind, they will never close, apart from Thursday afternoons.

The laundry shop. Ah yes, that smell of steam and the gathering of suspended coat-hangers. It still amazes me how we all have multitudes of coat-hangers in our wardrobes and yet none of us have ever bought any. Now we know how that is, as they all probably escaped and ran riot in search of new homes when they closed down the good old- fashioned laundries. They broke into our houses when we weren't looking and hid in our wardrobes.

For those of us who couldn't afford dry-cleaning, most of us I presume, there was always a trip to the launderette, and what a strange experience that turned out to be. It resembled a morbid doctor's surgery without the coughing and spluttering, an impossibility at this present time. Nobody ever spoke to each other as the clothes spun round and round like some warped fairground ride. Sometimes a tinge of aggression rose as people fought to use the tumble-driers before the person they had been ignoring for over an hour gate-crashed the orderly queue. Tempers raged and the fights weren't always clean fights, despite the location of the battlefield.

Dry cleaners had that beautiful, middle-class, steamy, almost arrogant fragrance, but launderettes just stank of working-class dampness, a cross between detergent and unwashed underwear. Every launderette employed a lady in blue overalls, yet no-one seemed certain of what she actually did and why she was there. We took our own packets of washing-powder and our own coins to get the machines spinning so there wasn't much she could do, other than stand around smoking enough Embassy cigarettes to collect sufficient coupons for a set of Pyrex dishes. She only needed to be there to open up at 7am and lock up at 7pm. The hours in between were a complete waste of her time, and don't forget this was a time when people weren't spending all day on their mobile phones, texting or building virtual reality farms. That wonderful pastime wouldn't appear for years. How the hell did we manage without the mobile phone? Answers on a postcard please. Postcard? Answers by email please.

A few doors along could be found the cobbler, the shoe repairers, and the quite erotic smell of leather that we loved even more as we became adults, obviously for different reasons.

Shoe repairers wore leather aprons, probably moulded or stitched together from unclaimed shoes and boots. Most of the shopkeepers had spectacles hanging from the tips of their noses like an old man in a Hans Christian Andersen fairy-tale. They sold tins of boot polish, laces, dubbin for football boots and watchstraps. They also sold tubs of whitener for plimsolls and odour-eater socks for people with smelly feet. They could put a new heel on a broken pair of high-heel shoes in a matter of minutes, along with various other services, but they never sold boots or shoes. It didn't seem right, a bit like a clothes shop only selling weaving looms.

To buy a new pair of boots, if the cobbler broke the news that your old ones had fallen into disrepair, you had to bid him farewell and make your way to the shoe shop, yet another retail outlet that now clings to the high street by its fingertips. Surely the shoe shop would win the fight against online shopping and supermarket once our battle has been won and we can all risk going out again? We all need to put something on our feet and, surely, we will need to try the things on to see if they are comfortable before parting with our hard-earned cash? Not so, I fear.

Mum bought stilettos, dad bought Oxford brogues to keep for best and my brother bought Chelsea boots after they had been popularised by The Beatles. I was thrust into a pair of sandals until I reached an age when I became utterly embarrassed to wear the damn things and bought a pair of Hush Puppies with my Saturday job wages. I'm not saying there is anything wrong with sandals, but red ones worn with white socks wasn't my idea of a good time at school. I looked like Mary Poppins' younger brother.

Without shoe shops we will never know what to buy our grandparents for Christmas. They are such a vital premises, places that tell our older relations they are not forgotten, so vitally important right now. They will have to come through this unscathed and re-open as we rekindle our relationships with our older relatives. It's been so long we probably won't recognise some of them.

I say unscathed yet I don't believe anyone in the country rushed to a shoe shop before they hid away in self-isolation, there would have been little point. None of us were going anywhere. Shopping for footwear has always been part of retail therapy but such a spree would have brought on waves of downright depression knowing we wouldn't be walking anywhere or showing them off down the local pub. Food was far more important than shoes.

I hate to be chauvinistic, but most women have at least ten pairs of shoes and just two feet, the same as men, so such shopping had to be top of the unnecessary list they mentioned in Downing Street. New shoes to wear on holiday? There are no holidays for the foreseeable future. New shoes to wear at a wedding? All weddings have been cancelled, a god-send to all skint parents right now. New work-shoes? Most people are working from home, toiling away in their carpet slippers and pyjamas. New football boots for the kids? Football is was out of the question for a while too until the government relented. That only left trainers to be worn down the gym. Hang on, gyms are out of bounds, one of the positives for me I have to admit.

The shoe shops continue to wonder about their futures as the enemy advances, ever closer, towards us all. As I say, they must survive as a matter of national importance to the unwanted older generation, and we hope they do, but they will have their work cut out. With the inability to go anywhere legally, unless we just happen to have a friend who is a high-ranking politician, or the advisor of a high-ranking politician, we are stuck indoors. One of the alternatives to walking around in new shoes is to baton down the hatches and read a few books in the hope of transcending oneself into safer pastures new. The other, far more outlandish, option, is to try and write such a book as opposed to reading one. A crazy idea, but speaking of books . . .

The bookshop, possibly the most sadly missed of all outlets as far as I'm concerned, had its own unique aroma too. Nowadays you can purchase the best-sellers from a supermarket, a fact that makes me wonder how they can ever become best-sellers in the first place if there are a lack of proper bookshops to swell the sales. It's all down to marketing, of course it is, and paying the supermarket for a place in their own unofficial book charts.

Book browsing has always been a wonderful pastime for me. Gone are the days when we experienced the joy of exchanging a book-token for a title you would never have bought with your own money. Gone are the days when we would buy a classic novel, which we would never read, purely to look intellectual when friends came to visit, little point now as none of us are receiving visitors. There's no point having a coffee table if you don't have any books.

All publications had a certain smell, be it the fragrance of glossy jackets or the musty smell of unread pages that had sat on the shelves for dozens of years. It all contributed to the bookshop experience, producing a beautiful smell that my nose may never witness again. William Shakespeare would turn in his grave if anyone had the foggiest idea where they buried him. Thomas Hardy's heart would be broken if they hadn't dislodged it from the rest of his body and buried it in Dorset once he no longer needed it.

Books paraded in supermarkets will never offer me the same idle time to stand and browse through pages like I used to. It can't all be about autobiographies of retired people of sport and soap stars, or romantic novels that blokes like me have no interest in whatsoever. Another Harry Potter book rolling off that nice lady's assembly line? It means nothing to me, I'm afraid. Why doesn't she flog her computer and give someone else a chance to have a best-seller? She's not short of a few quid. This book has every right to be a best-seller if other attempts by far better authors didn't get in the way and scupper my plans of selling millions of books, to say nothing of the film rights. Some books are simply crying out to be made into a film, this particular offering is gently sobbing rather than crying, yet I can definitely see someone as dapper as Tom

Hanks playing the part of me. There a certain resemblances if you have enough to drink.

My imagination now scans the various sections of the respected bookshops and it confirms we are, indeed, further up that creek without a proverbial paddle. There's a travel section, but nobody is going anywhere. A sport section although nobody is allowed to indulge in any sport in the way we used to. A cooking section at a time when almost all of our meals are coming out of the freezer with little regard for presentation. A gardening section when we're getting a little tired of endless hours in the garden. There needs to be a new section for books written by no-chance authors over seventy years of age. Now where did I put my Tippex?

To swerve away from the subject for a second, it's worth, at this point, noting how many high street shops gave so many celebrities their first jobs as they searched for their fame and fortune. George Michael, a personal chum of years ago, worked in the men's department of BHS, then known as British Home Stores, before he became half of Wham. Actress Glenda Jackson worked as a shop assistant at Boots the Chemist and Mick Fleetwood, founder member of Fleetwood Mac, worked as a window-dresser at Liberty's of London. To be mentioned alongside such household names I think I have the right to remind you again that I worked at Safeway as a shelf-stacker before they moved me across to the meat department.

It's nothing short of horrifying to imagine how many actors and musicians have lost their livelihood in recent times and will shortly need to return to the world of shop assistants to survive. With theatres closing and musical venues falling silent the time has come to swallow pride and earn a few pounds to pay the bills and fill stomachs. It may never have been expected by some of the more established performers, but it is something that simply has to happen. The major problem that faces such people is not just the closure of our theatres but also of shops where they will find such life-saving employment. Nearly every actress treading the boards has worked as a waitress at some time or another but now, finding such a post is slim. Restaurants and pubs will take on a new slant in the future as Perspex screens appear in such places. The actors and actresses were unlucky in the first place to lose their main source of employment, but they will need luck on their side to find an alternative way of making ends meet. They may need to look further than the high street.

That section of superstars, myself now sadly deleted, leads us nicely into the record shop, a meeting place where, by tradition, youngsters gathered on a Saturday morning, sporting their newest trendy clothes and hairstyles. Music blared out constantly and you could even listen to a new track before you considered buying it. Music booths, before headphones, were the perfect way to get close and meaningful to someone without them ever knowing your inner intentions. The excitement of buying a new record on the day of release was beyond words. The colourful sleeves of a 45rpm single, the long-awaited photograph on the front of a new album, it was all a major part of the Saturday morning experience for the young, not including me unfortunately, as my Saturdays were taken up with the food shop and football matches, football matches, I hasten to add, in front of swearing parents and not behind closed doors. That would come later to satisfy the financial concerns of the world's wealthy football moguls.

There was a top-twenty chart in those days, compiled purely by sales over the counter, not like today when they include all sorts of outlets including social media, downloads and other stuff that makes little sense to someone of my age. You had to sell a million records back then to reach the number-one slot, until the record sales industry collapsed and ten thousand sales would give you a sacred top-twenty status. Record shops have now been clobbered hard and hits are not recorded in the same way. I'm talking of long before cassettes, 8 tracks, CDs and downloads. It was just vinyl, much revered by record collectors of the time. They said vinyl had gone forever but it has enjoyed a resurgence in recent times, as have some of the artists of the 1960s who are still clinging to life. Actually, some who are no longer with us are still clocking up decent sales.

I can't quite remember when I began to venture into the record shop as part of my Saturday ritual. Come

to think of it, I can't remember what I did yesterday
afternoon apart from feed the birds.

My Saturday mornings changed with the passing
years and I was press-ganged into the weekly food shop.
At a younger age I looked forward to Saturday morning
pictures.
I remember all my adolescent days
and that's going back a few years now
There was Quatermass and Journey into Space.
Their voices still ring load and clear somehow
The Eagle and Black Jacks and everlasting strips.
Things I read like Biggles and newspapers round my
chips.
National Health orange juice and birthday ten bob
notes.
Idiot mittens with the strings around our throats.

I remember bags of coloured rubber bands
and streets that never had those yellow lines.
There were snake belts, mine was red and blue
and shops with metal Ovaltine signs.
Fags behind the bike sheds where my brother was a
Ted.
transistor radios smuggled into bed.
Cold winter mornings when the school milk froze.
third pint bottles yes I still remember those.

Saturday morning picture shows,
how we whistled when the film broke down.
Frozen Jubblies, Flying Saucers, Liquorice wood,

lead soldiers in a box for half a crown.
Having friends to tea, but never in the week.
Trying to ask a girl out, but forgetting how to speak.
Roy of the Rovers in his red and yellow shirt.
Building roads for Dinky toys in the garden dirt

Now I can but only look forward in vague hope of visiting a cinema sometime in the future, even though there's no rush as the movie industry has suffered the same closure as the rest of us.

It must be such a worry for those who have undergone face surgery and breast implants to look better on the big, silver screen, only to discover the pain and the cost of the pain were a complete and utter waste of time as the adored actors spend their time lazing by their swimming pools or strolling along their private beaches. Events that have now overtaken us all do not consider wealth or stardom. Money will obviously help with regards future survival, but you can't just buy your way out of this one. This wicked enemy attacking us does not accept credit cards.

Ah, I remember now, the visit to the local record shop followed a few years later than my first food shop and football days when I had far more time on my hands to grow up and find new interests. I never had much of a record collection, I have to admit that, but I still recall the colourful labels of a red Parlophone and a green Columbia. I would have also enjoyed the blue label of Decca if they hadn't turned The Beatles down.

Oh, such folly. We all make mistakes as the blind skunk who fell in love with a fart once said.

There was a haberdashery shop in my high street, but for years I never had a clue what they sold because I never went in there. I had no intention of buying a haber, whether it was dashing or not.

My next-door neighbour frequented the place with great regularity and I eventually began to realise the importance of the mysterious shop for those who spent their evenings sewing and making stupid hats for dolls. The shop sold fabrics, buttons, cotton of many colours and other tedious accessories such as hook things that held up curtains. I hate to be chauvinistic again here, but I reckon anyone who owned a haberdashery shop didn't have the foggiest idea what a bloke looked like, to say nothing of females under the age of forty, or thirty-five if I'm being generous.

I can only recall the shop window and nothing more, a window full of balls of wool of stunning colours, something that made me wonder why I had only ever seen white sheep when there were so many other coloured varieties, myself probably being the black one of my family, blissfully loafing around in fields far away.

I'm sure haberdashery shops have closed down in recent months which is really sad, even though it hasn't affected my own life in any way. I've never been short of buttons or ribbons, but any shop closure is sad.

I can only wish such shops a happy way forward in some shape or form or it will be the end of morris dancers as we know and see them today. Where will that jovial bunch of twinkle-toed, beer guzzling folk fans get their attire, their sashes, bells and ribbons? I sense yet another wonderful British tradition may be falling by the wayside as the bell-ringing legs of those fertility dancers stop moving and they shove their sticks on the bonfire, only after 6pm I hasten to add so as not to annoy the neighbours who you would think had far more important things to grumble about.

I'm afraid the future is all about a new, weird way of shopping in supermarkets, of which very few are situated in our high streets. For many months to come we will all be far too close to each other if we enter a small shop. It's a hard pill to swallow for someone of my age who has spent so many years wandering around with gay abandon, strolling in and out of shops without scrutiny.

My early food shops for my parents are way back in my murky past now, yet I lament and miss them so much. They were a major part of my life and it's sad the young children of today will be talking in years to come of a whole year of our lives we lost. Their children and their children's children will be reading of this time in history books, hardly believing what they will be reading. It's a sobering thought as our alcoholic intake has increased.

Chapter Eight – The Baker's Shop

Baker's shops have had their ups and downs over the years as more and more of the population work on their personal health and well-being, tending to give luscious cakes a miss. I find that whole thing ridiculous because if we didn't eat such wonderful objects we wouldn't need to go to the gym in the first place. No-one seems to realise that important point. They should sell huge cream cakes in gyms to ensure people return to lose yet more pounds.

I love baker's shops and we must not let them disappear from our high streets as we return to some sort of normality, despite their good or bad image. One minute they are health dens and the next you think you may put on weight when you walk through their doors. They were beginning to fight a losing battle years ago, as were most determined slimmers. More pounds on the stomach meant less pounds spent in the baker's shop as we all went on a bit of a health kick.

Do you ever wonder what happened to Mother's Pride, Sunblest and Wonderloaf? No, me neither, so let's just move on. Hang on, I've changed my mind. Let us not forget they were vital ingredients of a delicious bread and butter pudding when it was sacrilege to throw scraps of food in the rubbish bin. That said, we can now move on.

With the new bacterial intervention it seems the poor old baker is in for yet another excessive drumming when you hear of the amounts of flour and other bread-making ingredients that are being hoisted off the supermarket shelves as fast as the overworked stackers can put them on display. I tried to bake a few French sticks myself the other week, only to find one end stuck out of the oven and hit me in the face. I was never born to be a baker.

The time had come for novices to make their own bread, best they could, and I blame the excessive number of cooking programmes on television. Home-made loaves come in odd shapes and sizes, just like the people that bake them.

There was a trendy phase a decade or so ago when everyone bought each other bread making machines for Christmases and birthdays. Everyone who was someone owned a bread-making machine, big white things that cluttered up the kitchen. They were as essential as an unopened bottle of TCP in the first-aid cabinet. They were almost as common as Christmas cards on the wall. Very few recipients bothered to use the things and many ended up on the top of cupboards or at the back of a kitchen cabinet, and I mean the machines not the recipients. They never fetched more than a fiver at a car-boot sale. It is ironic that in more recent times we have, like them, all climbed up the walls or hidden ourselves away.

The one thing none of us can deny is that amazing smell of freshly baked bread. It's a beautiful aroma, far better than after-shave lotion, so it isn't unreasonable to feel people should create such a smell in their own kitchens.

Bakers have always dressed accordingly, looking more like hospital surgeons than shopkeepers in their white overalls and caps, and fair dos to them all. There isn't that much difference between someone who whips out your appendix and someone who flogs you a doughnut. Both options lead to a sore tummy.

As a small child I loved going to the baker's shop and being allowed to choose a cake from those on display, watching my mouth-watering choice being lifted from a tray by some large shop assistant with red, rosy cheeks who looked like she had personally tasted each and every offering before offering them to the general public. Most of the cakes involved cream in some way, be they vanilla slices, apple-turnovers or doughnuts, and although I enjoyed one, I would have gladly eaten half a dozen, fully aware of the impending gut ache and extra weight to my torso. I recall the joy of being allowed to choose my swag with my mother beside me, sometimes it being a custard tart or a Banbury cake.

Such conversations will now be difficult from here to eternity as people nervously keep their distance from one another. It would be difficult to keep six feet apart when discussing the various possibilities on offer. Imagine the noise of screaming kids shouting to their mothers six feet away. That in itself would be good reason to stay away from the baker's shop, either that or ban children from eating cakes unless it is their birthday. Unreasonable? The whole world has become unreasonable so I make no apologies.

The modern food shop doesn't always involve a trip to the bakers anymore as most supermarkets now have their own bakeries. Having said that, most items on offer are bread-based. There are bread rolls, French sticks and loaves of all shapes and sizes with continental origins. Cakes are on offer too, of course they are, but most are in pretty boxes and I, for one, miss the cheese cake, the one with those coconut-flavoured strands on the top that looked like albino worms, not to be confused with the modern cheese cake which is nothing more than a convenient way of disposing of stale digestive biscuits.

The colourful shop display of old may never return as it is in danger of giving way to pre-packed goodies, sold double wrapped in cling film and stinking of disinfectant.

It can therefore be argued that good comes from bad as we look after our calories, but surely that will never be the case. A yummy cake or two has to be on the culinary agenda after weeks of soup, baked beans and miles of spaghetti Bolognese during isolation. I yearn for the day when I can wave a hello to Mr Kipling and his fellow bakers and indulge in something I have missed for so long.

I don't really care about putting extreme amounts of weight on as I'm just glad to still be alive after what the wicked world has put us all through. We all deserve a celebratory overdose of sugar and I'll gladly be first in the queue, if allowed, when the sadly lamented smell of a bakery wafts through an open door in our new-found freedom. There will be no need for apologies or guilt as we all stuff our faces as a kind of thanksgiving. Americans have celebrated Thanksgiving for many years and it doesn't seem to have affected their weight. Hang on a moment. Come to think of it. maybe we forget about the cream cakes and I eat my words instead. I'm about to disagree with myself here. There's a fat chance of me losing weight while I sit in front of the television. I've eaten more biscuits in the last three months than all the inmates at Battersea Dogs Home have eaten in the last twelve, so I'm fully prepared to stop worrying about such side effects as heart attacks and enjoy the luxury of a cream-cake indulgence. Yes, it may affect my future exercise regime, but I could always become a Sumo wrestler.

There will always be hope for the bakeries of the future as there will always be a demand for wedding and birthday cakes as well as sausage rolls at funerals, cup-cakes at christenings and Victoria sponges at Golden Anniversary celebrations. They are all mouth-watering prospects for the future, even if not everyone at a funeral will be in a fit state to partake.

As I idle, I have been wondering how the term baker's dozen came to be. Most of us know a baker's dozen amounts to not twelve, but thirteen, but why is that so? We can always count on a baker, even if bakers can't count properly on their own fingers. Were they all useless at maths or was there some kind of ulterior motive?

It all goes back to mediaeval times, as do I most mornings, when a baker's supplies were measured in weight and not numbers. A law at the time stipulated that a certain amount of wheat had to go into each loaf of bread and if the baker's fell short of that quantity they were savagely beaten by sticks, another reason why we must protect the morris dancer and keep them active. To ensure such pain did not occur they baked an extra loaf and thus became the baker's dozen.

I shall close this chapter by sharing a thought that's relevant. What was the greatest thing before they made sliced bread? Time to move on to the farm shop.

Chapter Nine – The Farm Shop

Farm shops, now they are very interesting places I'm sure you'll agree if you have ever been bothered to visit one. They are shops that aren't quite shops, run by lavender scented people who aren't quite shopkeepers who aren't quite sure what they want to sell or what hours they should be open for business to members of the public who aren't sure what they are looking for.

To get the image of a farm shop in my head I think of myself on a school playing field wearing football boots, a crash helmet and a pair of swimming trunks while I wave a hockey stick around my head. There you go, there's a farm shop for you.

On the plus side they do welcome pets and prams and there is usually an area for tired shoppers to enjoy a cup of tea from a genuine china teapot. That can't be bad. A proper cup of tea never goes amiss when you are out and about, difficult as they may be to find.

I think we all share complete disdain when being served a cup of hot water with a teabag sitting in the saucer next to a small pot of pretend milk that's impossible to open without spilling on your jacket and a strand of a sugar capsule. That's not a cup of tea, that's an insult. Such behaviour never happened until people started going abroad for their holidays and the stupid idea was discussed upon their return. People who ran hotels and restaurants eavesdropped on those conversations and, as one, decided to adopt the idea for their own establishments. It came from hotels and restaurants overseas who couldn't be bothered to waste their time making their customers a decent cuppa when there was washing-up to be done. It becomes more common by the day and it is nothing more than a do-it-yourself tea kit. The tea bags used are the cheapest on the market and you never end up with a drink any darker than the rich-tea biscuit we all enjoyed before people went abroad for their holidays. A storm in a teacup? More like a light drizzle.

I now jump off the soapbox and return to the good old, harmless farm shop. Their offerings are varied to say the least. Home-grown vegetables, braces of not quite circular Victoria sponges, eggs from chickens and eggs from geese, houseplants and even fudge with a pallid photograph of their farm on the box. I wouldn't be surprised if there is one such shop, somewhere in this troubled country of ours, that sells gearboxes for second-hand Ford Fiestas and electric dog polishers, because anything goes in a farm shop.

Admittedly, I never ever saw such a unique, scatter-gun shop as I grew up in London, but I view them now as tiny garden centres, run by people who can't be bothered to buy large greenhouses. Yes, that's it, small garden centres without the gigantic stone statues that no-one in their right minds would think of buying, along with fruit trees too big to sling in the boot of the car. Strange places garden centres, they seem to excel in trying to sell you completely immovable objects such as heavy bags of sand, gravel and sheds that never fit on roof-racks of cars, to say nothing of plastic ponds, water features and giant koi carp that would never make the journey back to your home without suffocating or having a heron flying through the passenger-door window. It is so much easier to treat yourself to a tomato plant at the farm shop and get home as quickly as you can.

Paving slabs? No thanks. Giant pots and water-butts? No, I'll be fine without them. As for those ridiculous garden gnomes that are either fishing or having a piss, they are stupid, childish things that mock my love of Noddy books as I learnt to read, even if I was really too old at fourteen.

The food shop ritual rarely includes a visit to the farm shop for most of us and it didn't happen when I was a kid either. Nobody walks into such a place with a list of items to purchase given to them by their parents. I see it more as a spontaneous stop-off point, particularly for those in desperate need of a toilet or a nappy change, although I accept we're a bit too old for that sort of emergency. That doesn't mean we can forget the little ones during their moments of bodily crisis. Don't forget they are coming through this dreadful time too.

I can't begin to imagine how I would have felt if I'd been taken out of school for a few months. In truth, I can. There wouldn't have been enough champagne in the local off-licence to celebrate, even at such a tender age. Even if I'd been taken out of just maths lessons, and nothing else, I would have been happy, or maybe that doesn't add up.

The farm shop is also an opportunity for children to see rabbits and chickens dancing around in their natural habitat, as opposed to seeing them, desolate and defeated, in the butcher shop mortuary, something that can only be applauded. Also, credit where it is due, none of us would have the foggiest what an alpaca was, or what the thing looked like, if it wasn't for the good old farm shop. I'm not too well up on that sort of thing and I have to confess I thought a llama was a town in Wales, due to the double letters at the front of its name, until I was put straight by a visit to my local farm shop a couple of years ago.

If nothing else, all the above excluded, a visit to the farm shop involves a nice drive in the country and a pleasant walk from the car park to the shop itself. That explains why my mother never thought about sending me to such a shop. Firstly, I didn't live in the country and I never had a car of my own until I became a grown-up and secondly. The places didn't exist. It all makes sense now. Come to think of it, my father didn't have a car either, probably the reason why I was forced into food shopping at such a young age in the first place. Come to think of something else, there didn't really need to be any mention whatsoever of the farm shop within these pages did there? It has no bearing on my early shopping days. It only came into my head as there happens to be such an establishment near to where I now live, but to be honest I've never been there, even when I was allowed to wander around, before I became a home-bound, vulnerable old age pensioner on the brink of impending doom. I did know what a llama was really.

Maybe I will make amends when I reach my time of liberation because I have an old Fiesta in the garage in need of attention and they may just be able to help me out with a few spare parts. Failing that, I could always give an alpaca a stroke on its head and apologise to it for my ignorance. Oh yes, I'm going there if I'm ever allowed out for good behaviour. It's fifth on my list of must-dos.

Time to move on from this irrelevant chapter and return to other aspects of the food shop, a mission I undertook as a kid with great difficulty and now a mission I will be taking on in the future with even more difficulty, if at all, what with my aching bones that are now deemed worthless by the Government. I sense all sorts of obstacles will befall me as I try to get back into the swing of things, namely house arrest, on the spot fines for being old and the inability to stand in queues for long periods due to impending incontinence. Maybe I will need that farm shop to change my nappy after all. All I can say is that the farm shop is a welcome departure, diversion even, from the toil and drudgery of a normal day's shopping, so I make no apology for it being included. For a short time it has carried my brain back into the modern world.

I have no idea what a day's shopping will entail in they years that follow. It's such a scary thought and I suppose that's why all of us, no matter our age, wallow in the days that used to be. There are changes ahead that none of us wanted or predicted, so it is only natural to rest in the calm backwaters of yesteryear for safety and understanding during this dilemma. I feel there's nothing wrong with going backwards when there's not much to look forward to. We will all embrace the future and what it holds because we have no choice. I can only hope some of the little shops in the high street come with us all on our new journeys into the unknown.

Chapter Ten – The Coffee Shop

Let me state at the outset that I'm not as big a fan of the coffee shop as the rest of you. You think everyone loves a decent coffee shop, not me. My dislike stems from the fact that they sell coffee to take out. Coffee shops by tradition are nice places but they just had to go the extra nine yards and kill their own pleasant atmosphere by offering a take-out service, that Americanism again, for those who weren't attracted by a pleasant conversation in tranquil surroundings. No, coffee shops are far too busy for me.

The modern trend of mainly women, but occasionally men, walking around doing their shopping with a plastic cup of coffee in one hand, whilst clutching a mobile phone and a baby in the other, an annoyance I mentioned earlier, is an activity I would never have envisaged as a youngster as I went about my own shopping. I never walked around like that, I feel I had far more class. It's an annoying fashion statement that can lead to numerous trolley collisions in the supermarket and head-on crashes down an aisle, resulting in rushes to overcrowded hospitals at a time when they're up to their ears dealing with far more important issues. It's another selfish aspect of modern life that I choose not to be a part of.

Admittedly, it was a good few years after I had begun my food shop apprenticeship for my parents that I discovered the tranquillity of a coffee shop. Well, kind of. I say kind of because coffee shops didn't actually exist when I was a child. They came along later in my life when high streets became more international and a new trend came to be of stopping halfway through the food shop for a huddle around a table with other like-minded souls who needed to sling their carrier bags on the floor for a while and have a rest. It was all a bit Yankee doodle dandy but still far more civilised than walking around drinking and spilling the contents on small children in prams like mums tend to do in these more modern times. I'll give you that.

Years ago, children and young adults met up for a laugh and a bit of a chinwag. They didn't indulge in all this new-fangled hugging nonsense. We hugged our grandparents, an acceptable show of affection, but never our friends. That would have been such an off-radar thing for a child to do. We nodded to each other and that always seemed sufficient. Boys definitely didn't hug boys, whatever next? Boys pushed each other about before deciding if a fight was on the cards.

They weren't really coffee shops anyway, more the birth of the burger place. The first I recall was the Wimpy Bar. These places were founded in Indiana, The United States, way back in 1934. The first one cropped up in England exactly twenty years later, in 1954, at a traditional bastion known as Lyons Corner House in London, thought I'd look that one up for you. The Lyons Corner shop was a corner piece of the traditional English jigsaw. It's where old people went for a quiet afternoon just before they died.

Before you knew it they had burst onto the scene, like spots on a teenager's face, in every town and city around the country. They became a threatening alternative to the good old fish and chip shops as we all began to welcome skinny French fries into our mouths. There appeared to be, however, one fundamental difference between the two shops and I feel this could be a bit of an eye-opener.

Fish and chip shops of old never had areas where you could sit down and enjoy your food, with the exception of such places close to the beach at holiday resorts like Blackpool and Southend. Wimpy Bars invited you in to enjoy the new experience of sitting down for a while, enjoying your grub, rather than being hustled out of the way to allow the next customer in the queue to be served. Fish and chip shops learnt the error of their ways and adjusted accordingly, but it took a while and allowed the opposition to blossom.

In more recent times, today's world to be precise, queues in shops have become a thing of the past, as have sitting around cramped tables, so both establishments seem set for a rocky ride into the future. It remains to be seen who will win the battle but both fish and chip shops and coffee shops will need to change their approach and style of survival if they are to survive the abrupt changes.

I couldn't afford to visit a Wimpy Bar until I gained my first Saturday job in a high street shoe shop, before I became a Safeway shelf-stacker, and I still have the visual memory of my first Wimpy and chips. Milk shakes? Certainly not! Pepsi-Cola? Definitely not! Just Wimpy and chips with a friend. It seemed so grown up, the kind of thing my aunts and uncles did. They didn't actually, aunts and uncles weren't cool.

If you visit a modern- day burger place you will find all sorts of contents and burgers the size of dinner plates, or even satellite dishes if you're lucky. The meat, or vegetarian alternatives, is adorned with salad, mayonnaise, onions, pickled gherkins and tomato slices, along with other relishes that cascade onto your trousers as you take your second and third bites. A thousand island dressing? I couldn't name a thousand islands let alone eat one.

Early burgers were a round lump of processed something or other in a bun, with no allowance for those who didn't eat meat. They were tiny compared to the giants of today. It wasn't uncommon to wander up to the counter and buy a second one, something you would rarely see today in a modern fast food burger joint where considerate folk finish their meal, sling their trays in bins provided and get on with whatever they were doing. You rarely see such customers pondering on the thought of going back for seconds, a far cry from the school dinners ritual.

To my mind it was the Wimpy Bar that began the great burger revolution in Britain. I could be wrong, I'm not a historian, but I can't recall any similar place before they turned up on the high streets throughout the land. They were the foundation of high street socialising as we know it, I'm certain of that. I don't ever recall teenagers sitting in a greengrocery shop or a boot-repairers discussing a new movie or the latest album release by The Beatles. Socialising outdoors and along the high street had become the norm until the dreaded enemy took it from us. I stick by my beliefs, however inaccurate, that all trendy coffee shops in Britain came to be, thanks to the first burger bars of the 1950s. So you see, they weren't really coffee shops at all, but they served a similar purpose, particularly as a catalyst for what would follow, high street gatherings and conversations. Those were the days.

I never drank coffee as a child, it was never on my mother's shopping list. There were two main choices, Maxwell House or Nescafe, but we had neither in our house, only tea. Strangely, when I was old enough to hang out in coffee houses I still didn't drink coffee, preferring a glass of coke. I'd never been able to smell those roasted beans as I grew and so the lure came much, much later in my life, when I tried so hard to be a more sophisticated person.

Burger vans, an innovation in the 1970s, are nothing more than an extension of the seafood wagons that used to appear in pub carparks a few decades previously. They were nothing new. They fought with fish and chip vans for the prime slots nearest the pub entrance and they were popular with those who were so desperate for a drink they couldn't be bothered to cook dinner before they went out. That lot didn't drink coffee either, until the next morning as an aid to curing a stinking hangover.

So although this chapter has a coffee shop title, we have weaved our way through various food and fast-food outlets that weren't coffee shops at all. Very much like a food shop itself, we have meandered backwards and forwards along the aisles as we changed our minds or forgotten something we intended to sling in the trolley. There is nothing wrong with that. It happens, well, it happened once upon a time at least.

Just like a food shop, I'm not sure where this journey is taking me as things come into my head and I backtrack whenever I feel the need to. The changes in the high street were coming anyway, it's just that the enemy have speeded up the inevitable process. The changes in this book were bound to happen too as I had no idea what I would be writing about when I began, something I like very much. I made no notes, no written storyboard before I began. I know that's what most authors will do before they begin the hard work, but I needed to sit and let things come into my head naturally to re-live all the experiences I am sharing with you. I'm well I flit around all over the place but that's all part of the plan, to keep my brain active as I sit around at the moment doing absolutely nothing.

There is a great analogy when comparing the small retailer, battling against the odds, and a large supermarket that considers itself impenetrable. Just like fish in a pond, the little ones get gobbled up by the big ones and yet some of the small fry survive and make a success of their lives, hanging out under lily-pads as they wait for the next meal to come along. The big ones think they are safe until a heron turns up and bites them on the arse. What all of us have discovered in recent times is that we just don't know what lies in wait around the corner, waiting to bring our lives to a halt like some giant, motionless pike about to pounce.

Shopkeepers and manufacturers have all fallen victim to whatever it is that has come and attacked us all and it is a reminder that we are all fish swimming in that pond, hoping that nothing turns up and takes our normal existences away. We must not forget that some of the bigger fish were struggling in deep water under the strain of their own bodies long before this new wave of disaster, with many major stores closing their doors months before the attack.

Older people, such as myself and possibly older if they're still around, will sadly lament the passing of household stores, places synonymous with our growing up. Some of those fallen stores were part of my food shop, even my entire life in a funny sort of way. It is, therefore, fitting to mention them in passing as I continue my trip down memory lane towards the cul-de-sac I see before me. I'm about to mention established household names that we naively assumed would be with us forever. How wrong we all were as doors slammed like prison cells after the dinner hour.

We can't just blame the current crisis for the demise of some of those dinosaur establishments. The day of the department store had turned to dusk a few years ago as the new trend of shopping took hold. I'm not just talking of online shopping but the craving for specialist shops. When you think about it the art of shopping has turned full circle and returned to the days of my childhood. Even so, it is most fitting to mention the big boys in memoriam, those who believed they were too big to go under.

Chapter Eleven – The Big Fish

Back in the day, I occasionally put some time aside on a Saturday morning to nip into Woolworths for a look around at nothing in particular, because it was, indeed, a great shop for buying nothing in particular. They sold toys but with nowhere near the choice of a proper toy shop. They sold clothes, yet they were hardly trend-setters like their hip high street opposition. They sold paint, but the colour choices were minimal compared to those available in a hardware or paint shop. They sold electrical items, most were under their own trading name of Winfield, the middle name of the man who built the store from scratch. The more established brands had to be bought elsewhere, apart from the Morphy Richards hair-drier, a must for every girl approaching her first date. They sold stationery too, yet never enough to meet the needs of a home office worker. The only time they came out on top was when sweets were on the agenda. They knew how to sell sweets better than anyone else. Woolworths kept dentists in business for years, even if they couldn't manage to survive themselves through the changing habits of the public.

Basically, they were a gigantic bit-part concern that didn't really lead the field in anything, other than those sweets, and yet I loved Woolworths, it just had something about it and I felt a major part of my youth had died when it closed its doors for the last time. It's forever in my heart although the chances of me having a Winfield tattoo are zero.

As I say, the jaunt into Woollies was an occasional, most enjoyable diversion to fill some dead time between completing the food shop and going off to play football for the school. Woolworths were a huge concern and as safe as a bank, not a particularly great analogy these days I admit.

I recently heard someone describing banks as places that lend money to those who don't need it and take money from those who haven't got it. Oh, how short are the memories of those in the financial sector. We came to them as they waved the white flag of surrender and we received little thanks when the tables were turned. I digress, although with a certain amount of justified annoyance because I'm old enough to remember when people used to rob banks, long before banks started robbing people.

You could find a Woolworths in every single town and city in the country and, just like ourselves, we assumed they would be around forever. Oh, such a foolish assumption that turned out to be.

As a breather from gathering the family food I would often hover around the record department. Woolworths were so big and so damn important they even had their own record label called Embassy, a label that specialised in dreadful cover versions of songs that were in the top twenty. They were half the price of the original versions and the singers had half the talent. It can best be described as a kind of pop music for the poor. Even though I never had much money myself I never bought a single record on the Embassy label, it simply killed time to scan through the unknown names in the racks before I moved across to the sweets department. Now you're talking.

Their sweets counter, which I have already praised, was bigger than any local sweet shop and the whole area stank of pear drops and sugar. That was the strange thing about Woolworths, each part of the store had its own distinctive smell. The electrical goods section stank of burnt wiring and the paint section stank of white spirit along with the bodily smells of exhausted, unhealthy painters and decorators. So what's the story behind this giant of the high street that finally went bust?

Woolworths was founded by Frank Winfield Woolworth in 1852. The first Woolworth store opened its doors in that year, in New York, on 13th April. Despite what you think, despite my senior years, I was not there at the grand opening. The nice bloke was a kind of Quaker who liked to look after his family, with many of them involved in the building of the empire. It all went swimmingly well until the British stores, every single one of them, closed in 2009, thinking it could operate online only, a second plan that also went breasts north in 2015. 27,000 employees lost their jobs due to the financial crash and shock waves were felt in every one of Britain's high streets. If it could happen to Woolworths it could to anyone. High street shops never seemed in jeopardy until more recent times due to recession and an unforeseen circumstance that had just arrived without invitation.

The collapse followed an equal catastrophe that had occurred in 2001, the closing down of the clothes store C&A. I remember that store as well as I remember Woolworths. There were more button-down collar shirts than mods to buy them and more summer dresses than the days of summer could handle. They basically sold fairly plain clothes for fairly plain people, not a criticism as there were many fairly plain people around, but trends and styles changed and the mighty store couldn't keep up with the pace. From a young man's point of view, their off-the-peg suits were drab and their shirts were made for middle-aged office workers. What else did they sell that didn't exactly set my heart pounding? Socks, pyjamas, dressing-gowns, cardigans, pairs of braces and handkerchiefs with initials stitched on a corner. Now come on you younger people, would you have hung out there with your mates?

How did the Brenninkmeyer brothers start at the beginning?

They opened a shop in Holland that specialised in linen.

Then in 1922 to Oxford Street they came,

then Liverpool then Birmingham but the problem was the name.

Brenninkmeyer's thirteen letters had to change for sure

They'd need the longest shop in any city or town even longer than this particular line of the poem, a line that shouldn't really have this many words contained within as it affects the poetic flow…..

to shove the somewhat oversized family surname above the door

Think of a chemist shop and footwear for a clue.

If you've thought of Boots then unlucky my red herring's worked on you.

So Clemens and August Brenninkmeyer learned the error of their ways.

They took the initials of their names and renamed it C&As.

Another big store does spring to mind that wasn't particular cool being seen walking around with you mum. I'm talking of the Co-op, the good old Co-op, yet another premises that sold literally thousands of items and yet nothing much in particular. I'm well aware there are tiny Co-op shops still around, but once they were giant stores, like huge dinosaurs, and those former massive retail spreads went the same as the latter I'm afraid. They were the biggest store in the high street. Yes, exactly, they weren't shops, they were stores. You almost needed to hire a taxi to take your around all the different counters.

The Co-op paid dividends to customers, probably the inspiration and ultimate rise of the loyalty card of today. When anything was bought there the buyer would have to quote a number of, let's say membership or affiliation.

As I write I have no idea of the registration number of my car, letter alone my passport or National Insurance numbers. I struggle to recall my home telephone number because I haven't used it since the arrival of the mobile phone. When my home number rings I know it's someone who tells me I can claim on a road accident I was never involved in or that my house needs new windows. I never answer. Numbers are somewhere tucked away at the back of my grey matter and they don't venture forward very often. One number I hope doesn't appear any day soon is my own number, I hope that's not up like so many unfortunate others. However, I have never forgotten mum's Co-op number. It must have been etched on the inside of my eyelids. Was it that important? No, it made no significant change to my life whatsoever and yet it's still embedded in my brain.

I need to go back many years.

more than I wish to, it appears.

to when sherbet lemons stuck together

and we all chewed liquorice that resembled leather.

To the days when Wagon Wheels fitted wagons

(more about them mater)

when we used strange words like florins and flagons.

When David Nixon performed magical tricks.

447216

Further back than that we're going,

to the days of a certain Robert Owen.

In New Lanark this most co-operative gent

each day about his duties went.

Factories had a savage law
that affected lifestyles of the poor.
In my mind that number sticks
447216
A Woolwich bakery, some proclaim,
adopted the first co-operative name
and from these cheaper loaves of bread
the co-operative movement, like dripping spread.
The London Co-operative, I recall,
a great big shop, to one so small.
From Sensible shoes to Weetabix.
 447216
Where I bought a record for 6 and 8
or a record token for my mate.
Or the long grey socks, I wore at school.
Oh yes, and the curtain lady with the big long rule!
Broken biscuits in a big square tin
and purple stuff for a spotty skin.
Like the bingo caller's clickety clicks,
out came 447216
I don't know what the number did.
After all I was just a little kid.
'Divvy' is a word that springs to mind
but then I left it all behind.
Towards my teens I sped like a rocket
and things started slipping in my pocket
and a number not needed when someone nicks
Is 447216
So, the Co-op this is to you from me
as a long belated apology.

I suppose it's my own way of saying
sorry for leaving without paying.
Me and my mate were wanted stickers,
an east end scruffy pair of nickers.
Yet through it all that number sticks
447216

The writing had been on the wall for the big names for many years and for a while it seemed the smaller shops would spring back into life as the big boys fell around them. Many did and were doing quite well until disaster struck with epic proportions.

Meetings behind locked doors in Westminster have now forced shops to have locked doors too and reality is hitting hard. It is now more than likely that most locked doors will never be unbolted again as the high street footprint turns into a painful limp. Paying rent on premises that are no longer open and no flow of customers is a double recipe for disaster that will take some beating and good luck to overcome. For many the uphill struggle will prove to be far too steep. It's all very well saying shops can re-open on a certain date, but the debts have built up to such an extent that most will be incapable of picking up where they left off. I feel for them all. They will be short of stock and would have hoisted their credit limit to the top of the mast. It isn't looking too hopeful.

The big fish of today are now suffering like those before them with crippling rent charges, along with frightening arrears payments and everything seems so uncertain as a few more, a very few more, green shoots begin to sprout, just like they told us a few weeks ago during their daily briefs from Downing Street. Reality is far more important than happy pills as not just the over 70s, people like me, feel more and more vulnerable by the day,

The first warning sign came when statistics showed over thirty-per-cent of Christmas shopping last year had been done online, sad figures of progress in my opinion. As a child I loved Christmas shopping, counting up my pocket money and walking around the shops thinking of things members of my family would appreciate. Sometimes I would be inspired by something on display in a shop window and I'd count the coins to see if it was affordable. I was never a Christmas Eve shopper like some people. I walked the high street for a good few weeks before the festive period, searching out gifts and I absolutely loved it.

To an old fogey like me online shopping just isn't the same and it never will be the same. No way can it erase that memory. Wrapping presents was another thing altogether, I wasn't any good at that sort of thing, but some nice shopkeepers would do that too if you asked nicely. Online shopping is no good if you don't have the slightest idea what you're looking for and that's where the high street should have won the day, but it just didn't happen.

My schoolfriend, Kevin, came from a very poor family and he was always flat broke, so much so that he did all his Christmas shopping by shoplifting. The arrival of online shopping would have killed his giving of presents stone dead, an unreasonable outcome I would suggest. Speaking of stone dead, poor old Kevin died years ago and so he never had to adapt to the modern form of shopping that made no allowances for stealing. He was always getting himself into trouble, another problem with shopping online for him would have been the need to give an address for delivery. Kevin always gave a false address and old habits die hard. There would have been no Christmas present from Kevin this year, even if he were still around.

The first retail collapse I recall was Littlewoods once the biggest family-run chain in the country. I suppose I had an affinity with them because my dad did Littlewoods Pools every Saturday and the company kept him buoyant by giving him the opportunity of becoming a multi-millionaire. If he ever managed it he kept it a closely guarded secret, so much so I was never given a rise in my pocket money and we never moved out of our council flat.

Then came the demise of Toys R Us a couple of years ago, a store that looked as safe as dolls-houses. Once again, a warning shot had been fired across the bows of the retail world. I wouldn't call it a good old high street brand anyway as they turned up in just about every out of town shopping centre in the country, but yes, it was fair warning just the same. Maybe it's fall from grace will allow the small toy shops to have another crack of the whip in times to come.

As I look back at my final walk down the high street before I shut myself away it's quite an emotional affair. I didn't realise at the time I was waving goodbye to so many shop fronts I would never see again. It made me think longer and harder of the other shops that accompanied me through my childhood. Most shops are now boarded up and window-cleaners are using sanders instead of sponges, but once every shop in the high street stood proud with their own traditions and stories to tell. For that reason I have to continue on my backward journey. It may be a history lesson for some, but it was a reality to me.

Chapter Twelve – The Off-Licence

This chapter will only appeal to those of you over eighteen years of age, as the rest of you won't have a clue what I'm writing about due to legal reasons that prevented teenagers becoming alcoholics before they even got a job. It was a very fair law they passed as it had to be so bloody unreasonable to expect teenagers to have drink problems before they had wage packets that enabled them to buy alcohol in the first place. You need personal identification and proof of age to buy anything in such a shop, even though no-one has asked me for such identification or such proof for over sixty years. I now have to provide identification and proof that I am not over 18, but over 70, an age that allows me to join a special queue on Tuesday mornings.

There must have been so many last-minute trips to the off-licence recently as people turned to the odd tipple to help them get through such a tough time ahead. Perhaps the thought of a break in the risk of drink- driving has something to do with it, to say nothing of pubs shouting last orders for a considerable time too. Whatever the reason, off-licences experienced one hell of a boom phase before everyone went into their enforced hibernation. I must say that one of my own final checks before locking my door was ensuring there was enough alcohol in the cupboard to stop me going stir-crazy. Of course, I'm not advocating drink to be a sensible solution to any dilemma but there are times when it can help. An apple a day may well keep the doctor away but what do you do when you can't get to the shops and buy any apples? That's my excuse anyway.

I'm not a serious drinker. I don't mean I don't laugh lots when I'm enjoying a swig, but I do not drink to excess. Despite the admission, I decided I needed enough to see me through watching countless movies on television or sitting in the garden on a warm evening watching flies and other insects bite my legs.

Ants like a good drink too. Put a can of lager on the grass and they are swarming all over it by the time you've eaten a bag of crisps. On the subject of crisps, a scientific fact I've discovered is that ants prefer plain to cheese and onion and blackbirds don't care what flavour you toss at them. As my dad used to say, every day is a schoolday, another fact I knew wasn't actually a fact when he told me that on a Saturday or a Sunday, which weren't schooldays at all. I chose to keep my lip buttoned rather than be subjected to a painful, unfair clip around the ear for telling him of his error. He was never wrong so there was no point.

The whole science of nature thing is an interesting point, even if it is tucked away in a chapter relating to an off-licence. Mother Nature, the most respected of non-drinkers, has blossomed over the last few months, choosing not to inform its other forms of life that something strange is going on. For instance, the ozone layer over Australia has more or less mended itself, magnificent news and worth the raising of a can of lager, the coral reef seems to be righting itself a little, worth the raising of another can of lager and great news for door to door salesmen who sell sponges. The air is now much clearer with the cessation of air travel, well worth the raising of a third can of lager. As I've always said, if God had wanted us to fly he would have given us tickets. Whilst our worlds have deteriorated and sent us in fantasy flights towards the off-licence, the rest of the world, in its other forms, seems to have taken it all in its stride and made some things better for the planet.

The things that live in my garden don't seem to be affected in the slightest by what's happening either and that may well be because they too are enjoying a drop in air pollution. The birds seem to be singing louder and flapping their wings harder, especially annoying pigeons first thing in the morning, and insects seem to be far busier than usual. None of them seem to have a drink problem like the ants. They're too occupied with other things to just lay on the lawn and get drunk.

I accept it may well be coincidence but, at this time of mass uncertainty, it may be true that some sort of good is coming out of this global dilemma. I have the impression that creatures great and small think it their right to be spending more time in the garden if we are doing the same. It's difficult to find good in bad sometimes but, just maybe, nature has benefitted at long last from the lapse in destruction caused by us humans. It definitely seems to be that way in my busy back garden anyway. There are no white, aeroplane trails across the sky and the traffic seems to be quieter too as those who dare to sneak out try not to make too much noise revving up their engines. Even boy racers seem to have stopped stealing cars and gone back to playing war-games on their computers. Yeah, all things considered, I sense a few positives in so many negatives.

Early blossom has appeared on the trees and flowers are popping their heads up far earlier than usual as the closing down of the planet coincides with the opening up of so many beautiful plants as we experience the warmest springtime on record. Nature may well have a point because warm weather normally leads to barbecue smoke and the cremation of sausages and burgers, yet there are no such evils climbing skywards into the evening sky this particular year. Everything seems purer, other than the very thing that makes everything else seem purer, if that makes sense. I had to read that line again myself, but it does make sense if you read it slowly. Another bonus is the increased levels of ultra-violet, a thankful helping of vitamin D, an ingredient that fights the nasty visitors to our bodies.

Barbecues contribute little to the intake of vitamin D but they definitely contribute to a higher intake of cold beers and chilled wine. This in turn will increase the intake of units and with our cars out of action it encourages us all to stay fit and healthy by through rugged walks to the off-licence. Utter boredom must have shot the numbers up even further. Owners of off-licences would have been rubbing their hands with glee if they had been allowed to get hold of our wallets and credit cards. Unfortunately for them, that isn't the case.

Off-licences are yet another trade hit by the rising popularity of supermarkets over the past couple of years during this double-whammy, what with their cut-price offers, but it didn't seem there would be enough alcohol to go around as the bug bit so, like other shops mentioned, they seem to be in with a chance of survival. Boxes of ale and lager fell out of the supermarket doors and into the boots of cars, an action the excessive drinkers themselves would not be worrying about, what with the empty roads. Lemonade is all very well and thirst-quenching on a beautiful spring evening, but heads are spinning as we try to make sense of things. Although alcohol makes our heads spin even faster it acts as a companion for so many of us at times of uncertainty and loneliness such as now. My head spun last night, only because I tried to ram a corkscrew into a screw-top and cut my finger.

Both my parents were non-drinkers with the exception of my mother's birthday glass of sherry and a snowball at Christmas. My dad didn't touch the rotten stuff, not even a cheeky shandy. He didn't survive the war to get a nasty headache in the mornings. That being the case I never set foot in an off-licence until I had left school. The only drink on top of our sideboard at

Christmas was the aforementioned Harveys Bristol Cream along with a bottle of advocaat that mum drowned in lemonade.

Sometimes, when you are writing a book such as this one, you need to refer to the spellchecker to make sure you don't appear illiterate. Advocaat is such a word that sent me scurrying to my mobile to double check its accuracy. It's a Dutch word and the Dutch use different words to us. It's called Dutch.

Advocaat never looked that inviting. It was made from eggs and it glared a bright yellow, like a load of custard shoved in the wrong bottle. It makes me proud that I couldn't spell such a ridiculous drink.

We never had beers or cider on that sideboard. I never tasted beer until I went to college and it was whilst a student I made up for lost time, so, if I'm being honest, it's difficult for me to compare the old off-licence with the new.

The meaning of off-licence is that alcohol can be purchased in the shop but must be consumed off the premises. I think most of us know that and it applies to other shops too. I've never seen a shopper buy a nice piece of beef in a butcher's shop and cook a wholesome Sunday lunch before they walk out the door. I've never seen a dear old lady buy a few balls of wool and walk out the shop with a new cardigan.

Off-licences were always closed on a Sunday, something to ensure heavy drinkers would not skip church and go to confession. It wasn't until 1994 that such shops were allowed to open on a Sunday. Once again, that wasn't any big deal as I can't remember a single shop during my youth that opened on a Sunday anyway, apart from the newsagents, a shop I shall visit in the next chapter as I was always sent for a Sunday paper by my dad. Nowadays, everything is open on a Sunday. There are football matches, motor racing, endless car-boot sales and theatre shows. Sundays were a far more respected and religious twenty-four hours back in the day when I was a choirboy. Now, with the exception of the deeply religious it's just another day of the week, even if you can get a free swig of wine and a slice of bread if you bother to go to communion. I've had a fair few Sundays pass by recently and I didn't even notice they had come and gone. It's so weird how Saturdays and Sundays used to have something special about them. They sort of turned up as processional leaders of a new week of five ordinary days. Now they are nothing but part of the same old seven days. Weeks have turned into tedious months and months may well turn into tedious years if we're not careful as we plough our way onwards and sideways.

There was no such thing as an expensive wine in the old-fashioned off-licence, no grand collection of squashed grapes from exotic countries around the world trodden or trampled on by experts. I didn't know where Chile was, let alone the fact that they made wine there. I just thought it was such a strange name for such a hot country, I knew nothing more than that. California was where film stars came from, not winegrowers. When I went to Saturday morning pictures, most of the film stars rode horses. Just imagine the damage they would have inflicted on a budding vineyard. There was just one plain and simple red wine, an equally plain and simple white wine and that was the end of it. You drank white wine with fish and red wine if you wanted a stinking headache the next morning. If you mixed both together, fifty-fifty, you had rose, a more delicate drink for older relatives. I think all the red types came from France, as did French people and all the white equivalents came from Spain, as did bullfighters and bank robbers on the run.

In the old days we never had lorries driving all around Europe and further afield just to pick up thousands of bottles of this contraband from different nations who had decided to start growing the stuff so they could understand the writing on the labels. French isn't the easiest language to comprehend, unless you are French of course, and those white labels with tiny gold lettering don't help matters. Red or white, French or Spanish, the choice was yours. If you are about to dabble for the first time in the understanding of beautiful wines to twitch your nostrils, you will discover that bottled wine is slightly better than the canned variety. It's very rare to find a decent vintage wine from a hundred years ago, sitting in a can. Take that from someone who knows exactly what they are talking about. I have a vintage tin of baked beans in my cupboard and they're only six years old.

I own up, my recall may be inaccurate due to the fact, already mentioned, that I never set foot in an off-licence, but my young eyes saw the bottles on display in the window on many's the occasion so that is the conclusion I came to, probably wrongly but who cares?

Wines and spirits it said above the shop window. My parents didn't drink wine and didn't believe in spirits so I was never sent there, which makes you think this particular chapter has been a complete and utter waste of time. The newsagent I knew lots about and remember well, so it's time to move on and allow me to write with some sort of authority.

Chapter Thirteen – The Newsagent

The newsagent I know all about because they gave me my first ever job, as a paper-boy. I didn't last long when I realised newspapers had to be delivered first thing in the morning and not just in the evening, but at least I gave it a go.

Paper-rounds could last anything up to two hours which meant getting to the newsagents at six o'clock in the morning before heading off to school. My little body didn't take too kindly to such a ruling. My brother had a paper-round too, but he also had a bike, so his round was far quicker than mine. He would be back home eating his porridge by the time I'd walked the first couple of streets with tired feet.

The heaviest papers by far were The Daily Telegraph and The Times, but fortunately nobody where I lived read either. Many couldn't even read at all so they chose the papers that contained the most pictures. The Daily Mirror led the league table for sport, with many in my area not bothering to spare a glance at the first dozen pages. It was a case of straight to the back pages to discover the latest football or cricket news. It's remarkable to think that cricket was once as popular in Britain as football, well in England anyway. I can't really speak for the Welsh, mainly because I can't speak

Welsh. Scottish people played the odd game of cricket when they weren't tossing cabers and the Irish had a sport of their own that contained rules that no-one really understood other than the Irish, although I'm not too sure the Irish knew the rules either. Football with hockey sticks and rugby without the tackles. They invented it and surprisingly they remain the only nation that bothers to try and play it.

Football seasons finished on Cup Final day, the first Saturday in May and when I say they finished, I mean they finished. No sooner had the silverware been lifted than the first over was bowled to welcome in the cricket season. It usually rained but they still got dressed up in their whites in case of a break in the weather. Football was never mentioned in the newspapers again until the end of August when everybody had grown sick to death of cricket. Despite the closure of the football season it never affected the circulation of a newspaper. There were cricket legends way before Ian Botham and sport-lovers wanted to read all about them. County cricket scorecards were added to the back of The Daily Mirror, something you don't see these days. Football moved on and became a mega-rich industry with some players earning half a million pounds a week, whilst cricket moved on and used a white ball on occasions instead of a red ball. They were no longer of equal status. England were playing cricket in The West Indies and West Indians were playing football in England.

This is the year when the football season hasn't finished in May. It's become a sport that has organising bodies as confused as our politicians. The current situation has seen football take a back seat of importance with no games played for several months, only to return with clubs playing fixtures behind closed doors. That only goes to show that the game is run for the sake of the wealthy club owners and sponsors and not for the true football fan who will continue to be denied watching such spectacles for a longer period. My own rubbish team have enjoyed a wonderful last three months, not losing a single game.

The newsagent had a distinctive smell of news print, a fragrance that hit you harder than the smell of pipe tobacco when you walked through the door. For the short time I was a paper-boy that stink used to smack me in the face every morning at a time when I should have still been in bed. My granddad smoked Old Holborn so I was already familiar with that pungent aroma when I visited him.

The two heaviest deliveries were Exchange and Mart on a Wednesday and the Radio Times the following day. All these years on, admittedly with unimportant inaccuracies, I can recall the order of how my bag was packed by the newsagent and with which publications. There was Woman's Own, Bunty, TV Times, although I'm not too sure about that date-wise, Woman's Realm, Sunny Stories, and then there were the comics. Now this was the perk for the paper-boy.

I never had to buy comics because as soon as I'd got round the corner I would sit down and read how Roy of The Rovers had scored a hat-trick within the pages of The Tiger and which planet Dan Dare had travelled to via the pages of The Eagle. I laughed at Biffo the Bear and Lord Snooty and his pals in The Beano a couple of years before Dennis the Menace came onto the scene. I never read The Dandy for some reason before I progressed to The Valiant and The New Hotspur, far more grown-up publications. Do you ever wonder what kind of grown-ups thought up this kind of subject matter? They must have been adults who still wore short trousers, sucked gob-stoppers and didn't change their underpants for a week.

Of all the publications the one I longed to see the most was Charles Buchan's Football Monthly. Being a football fan, with the outside chance of becoming a professional footballer, or so I thought, I awaited it's arrival each month. The magazine contained full-page colour photographs of the top players and I have to confess many copies of Football Monthly were delivered with the odd page missing so I could add to the gallery on my bedroom wall at no cost.

Every Friday I delivered The Angling Times, another interesting periodical for a young lad who had just taken up luring fish from dis-used gravel pits. It's fair to say my short reign as a paper-boy didn't come without its benefits, it's just that I couldn't get up in the mornings, unless of course I was going fishing or travelling to a school football match where I pretended to be one of the international players stuck on my bedroom wall. Hypocritical or what?

The newsagents has changed dramatically since my childhood. There were no blokey magazines on the top shelves like there are today, apparently, and no such things as home improvement tomes or magazines featuring yachting. The newsagents sold mainly newspapers along with other essentials such as sweets and cigarettes. From the age of five I could pop in and buy my dad's tobacco without the shopkeeper checking to see if I had nicotine stains on my tiny fingers. Of course it was for my dad.

There was once a time, before people knew better, when most of the population over the age of seven and a half enjoyed the odd cigarette. Both my parents smoked, all my neighbours smoked and I have feeling even some pets enjoyed a quick fag too or they wouldn't have called them dog-ends.

Cigarettes came with incentives to buy in the shape of coupons, as in the case of Embassy and Kensitas, collected by the lady in the laundrette or cigarette cards that could be collected and stuck in albums. Unlike today the packets were attractive, far more attractive than what lived inside them. Nowadays, all packets look the same, black with a dreadful photograph of some sick person and a government health warning blazed across the front. Whether you are a smoker or not you cannot deny some of the packets were real works of art.

Players Navy Cut had the picture of a salty sea-dog sailor on the front. There was Capstan Full-Strength, a fitting title for a cigarette that need a full quantity of strength to survive the coughing they used to bring on. Designers must have toiled through the night, puffing away, coming up with packet artworks to entice a smoker to buy. There were Guards, a white packet with a red stripe and a black top, just like a Grenadier Guard during Trooping The Colour. My Auntie smoked Piccadilly, another white packet but with a gold medal on the front, hanging from a blue ribbon, as if the nasty habit warranted some kind of recognition. The favourite of the working classes were Weights and Woodbines. There came a time when many smokers went on a health kick and turned to Consulate, a menthol variety, a bit like a polo mint without the painful crunching of the gums. Many gentlemen also chose to smoke a pipe, like Popeye without tins of spinach tucked inside their shirts.

Pipe-smokers were mainly chaps who had been at sea for far too long to know what was good for them. They puffed pipes as some kind of respectful gesture to the ships they sailed on that blasted filthy black smoke out of funnels. Other pipe-smokers included architects at the drawing board, politicians on the canvassing trail, painters, radio announcers and cricketers waiting in the pavilion to take to the crease.

It may be an unacceptable habit these days, but there seemed to be an artistic attachment to smoking and the departure of the bright packets is one that is missing in this new world of personal health and social etiquette. To be honest, there was never anything worse than to walk into a room where a man sat puffing at his pipe with the smell of tobacco filling the room. It wasn't a pleasant experience.

Inside the newsagents I always preferred the sweets area, the mini-Woolworths I described earlier. That's where I tended to hang out, for obvious reasons, while the newsagent went out the back to load my delivery sack. The recollection of such a shop made me turn to rhyme some years ago now as sweets and associated items of such bygone days cluttered my brain.

There were; Fruit salads, black jacks, marshmallow shrimps
Jubblies, bazookas and spangles and imps.
The kid in the class who spoke with a lisp
Boxes of Brocks on November 5th
The Saturday classified pink with the scores
Dad checking his homes his aways and his draws
Knock down ginger banging on doors
Does anyone remember love hearts

Tortoises sleeping in cupboards for months
Catching the chicken pox measles and mumps
Dennis The Menace and Korky The Cat
Desperate Dan in his ten gallon hat
Pineapple chunks, strawberry pips
Kissing a girl who you love on the lips
Bottles Of Tizer all taking sips
And washing up bowls full of tadpoles

Danger Man was terribly hip

Like 77 Sunset Strip
No Hiding Place, Dixon too
Captain Pugwash and Mr Magoo
Remember how his sight was short?
Here's an insignificant thought
How come the fugitive never got caught
After all those years on the run

So that the barber could cut your hair
You sat on a plank on the arms of a chair
The barber said to the grown up men
Is there something you need for the coming weekend?
A packet of three they usually said
Which went completely over my head
Til I got a girl called Jenny in bed
And I could have done with one them

One potato two potato
Three potato four
Five potato six potato
Seven potato more
Palm toffees, scoobedoos,
Reginald Bosenquet reading the news
The Animals House Of The Rising Sun
A five minute single at number one

Palma Violets, jamboree bags
Round the bike sheds puffing at fags
Flashy cars like e type jags
Though we only had a Cortina

Down to the Army and Navy store
For things worn in the second world war
Duffle bags, duffle coats
Idiot mittens with string round our throats

Sooty and Sweep, Beyond our Ken
The Michelin Man and Bill and Ben
Do you remember conkers when you
Made them hard in the oven
Flying saucers and liquorice wood
William Tell and Robin Hood
The Dandy the Beano The Beezer as well
Bing Crosby going well on shell

Putting a tiger in your tank
Watching tales of the riverbank
Rin Tin Tin, Lassie and Hank
Parker and Lady Penelope
Esso key rings, packets of Tide
Where you were when Kennedy died
Tiger Nuts, sherbet dips
Collecting cards from PG Tips

Penny bangers and two-penny chews
Elvis Presley in GI Blues
Wearing painful sensible shoes
Woodbines washed down with cream soda
Being scared of catching the pox
Hush Puppies and luminous socks
Chalk on the blackboard a horrible noise

What did you do with your Dinky Toys?

Swizzles refreshers and cola cubes
Remember when Zubes were good for your tubes
Girls in class developing boobs
And making masks for the smog
Double Your Money with Monica Rose
The very first record of Status Quo's
Radio Caroline, Tom Thumb,
Little Plum your redskin chum

Colonel Mustard, the Reverend Green
Whatever happened to Hope and Keen
Remember the ad for Ovaltine
Sheriff's badges and snake belts
Blind dates, roller skates
Bachelors Senior Service and Weights
Semolina they served at school
And clothes you lost at the swimming pool

It was always a sock you managed to lose
Even worse you lost one of your shoes
Going home and breaking the news
And getting a clip round the ear
Michael Miles, Provident cheques
Remember those National Health type specs?
The boys had brown the girls had pink
Remember those great big bottles of ink

Squints splints and Murraymints

Knackered lighters that needed flints
Waterloo Sunset by The Kinks
And going to work on an egg
Remember the horrible ad for Tunes?
Wearing flairs and pairs of loons
Five stones, we called them gobs
Bootsie and Snudge and Saturday jobs

Third pint bottles of milk
I Spy books and Acker Bilk
Thinking your hair was as smooth as silk
When you covered it over with Brylcreem

There was a time when it seemed there were over two hundred different varieties of Spangles alone, my favourite being tangerine, and Palm Toffees had numerous flavours too.

The final perk as a paperboy was the presentation of a Wagon Wheel along with my weekly earnings on a Friday evening. This was a time when Wagon Wheels fitted wagons, huge things that almost had to be eaten with two hands. Nowadays they are nothing more than little, round chocolate objects, but I remember when they were a challenge to take on. They were so big you could pass them around the classroom and let others take a bite around the rim and still have enough to give you a stomach-ache. So, every Friday I went home with my Wagon Wheel and my money and I felt a sense of real achievement. It turned out to be a rather short experience as part of my youth but it's still in my head.

I have no idea if newspapers will continue to decline in popularity. With people shut in at home it must have dented sales to commuters on buses and trains, to say nothing of papers collected by old age pensioners as they took their morning stroll with their pet dog. Those categories must have represented a fair percentage of newspaper sales and I sense that many would have grown familiar, during these troubled times, of keeping up to date with the news through their tablets and mobile phones, possibly with the exception of the old age pensioners who have other tablets for other reasons if they managed to secure an appointment with their doctor.

What if magazines went out of business? How would any of us endure that painful wait at the dentist without some two-year-old magazine for car enthusiasts being on the table in the waiting room to take our minds off what was about to happen to our gums? The same can be said for the doctor's surgery. Before our imposed exiles we all waited up to midday for our eleven o'clock appointment, reading an old edition of Country Life, a magazine that confirmed we were all financial failures in comparison to how the other half lived. Well, it's all changed now and everyone is heading towards the precipice of financial failure at their individual levels. Blimey, I've read that some poor people are having to sell their own private islands. That could have been a hell of a story to wrap around a piece of fish and chips, a completely different arse to Sir Bobby Charlton's imprinted on a piece of cod.

The thing is there are no longer the traditional fish and chip shops around to take our newspapers and magazines to wrap the food in. Dustmen, or whatever they call themselves these days, ah yes, refuse disposal officers, err, yes dustmen, they won't take the things away either if you happen to sling them in the wrong bin. Phew, what with that and what's going on in Syria.

It all gets more confusing by the day and there seems to be little light at the end of the tunnel. The days grow ever longer, the tunnel stretches further into the distance and our levels of boredom and patience are being stretched to the limit as our levels of optimism decrease at an equally alarming rate.

Personally, I would hate to see the newspaper disappear into or on to the computer screen. Newspapers are tactile objects that can be browsed, tucked under the arm on the walk to work, or rolled up to smack an annoying housefly on the head. They can be piled into a bundle for no apparent reason or ripped into shreds to allow model railway enthusiasts to build hillside scenes. Surely, we can't just let all that disappear as though it isn't that important?

Chapter Fourteen – The Sweet Shop

I have already mentioned my favourite section of the newsagents that sold sweets, along with details of my complimentary Wagon Wheel so you probably understand, strange as it may seem, I didn't visit the local sweet shop too often, something my teeth have been thankful for in later life. The odd trip to Woolworths sweet counter and the sweet-stealing at the newsagents seemed to suffice.

I don't need to stack up right now with piles of sweets to get me through the current crisis as I have a funny feeling my sweet tooth met the magical tooth fairy under my pillow many years ago, so I can easily go without, as I had done for many years.

Every Saturday morning I would nip into the sweet shop on my way home from playing football for a different reason. I bought a cold drink to quench my thirst and sometimes I would buy bubble-gum because they attached cards of footballers. Other than that I wasn't all that bothered with other things that adorned the shelves. I seemed to buy more bubble-gum the closer I came to completing my set of cards. There was nothing worse than missing out on a Middlesbrough footballer I had never heard for the sake of developing lockjaw and diabetes just to get hold of him. By the time

I found him I had a rotten tooth and put on two-stone in weight.

Today, one is able to buy sweets in a supermarket along with the rest of the food shop, by-passing the sweet shop as I had more or less done myself in favour of the newsagent.

Sweets were weighed and placed in little white bags and they had to be eaten quickly before the contents stuck to the bag and kids walked around spitting out tiny pieces of paper. Supermarkets have tried to emulate that experience by having displays that resemble changing-room lockers with the fronts removed. Tiny plastic shovels are on hand to pile the mixtures into much bigger bags to ensure bigger profits. Not content with that, they designate a whole aisle to bars and boxes of chocolate, peanuts, all sorts of nuts actually, bags of pre-packed sweets, marshmallows and if that isn't enough there is a huge selection of kids' sweets on the bottom shelf, in sight of the little ones who scream their heads off if their wishes aren't granted. My future major food shops, should they ever happen again, will never include such childhood treats for reasons stated if I ever dare to queue up and venture in.

My own current food shop? Yes, you read right. Good news, I have been told I can venture to the shops more openly now, but only for essential items. The government have allowed the re-opening of car showrooms as the first retail outlet to be back in business since lockdown. Wow, I can't begin to imagine how many of us are about to nip off and buy a brand new Range Rover in this current financial climate, only for it to sit motionless, waiting until we're allowed to drive wherever we wish, whenever we wish. Which clever government adviser came up with that smart idea? I wouldn't be surprised if it isn't some government adviser who has a brother who flogs cars or a relative who lives far away. A car showroom is a truly important point of sale. Well done you guys who make such important decisions. I've just realised that a new car is one of the rare items not available in a supermarket.

I can't think of many other essential items that cannot be bought in the supermarket, thus confirming the pending demise of all smaller shops that cannot buy in bulk, causing them to keep their prices higher so as to make some kind of profit. Of all the shops mentioned so far in this book, because of the supermarket, there isn't one that would affect us big style if they close the doors for good and that's a desperate admission for the retail sector. There are the opticians, the key-cutters, the clothes shops, the off-licence, the chemist and the butcher and even the shoe shop. All their specialist goods are now available under one giant roof.

When doing an important food shop in a supermarket, as has been the case in the past few months, it's difficult to find the food tucked away with the greetings cards, saucepans, lottery-ticket counters, games and puzzles and the TV and DVD section. It surely doesn't bode well for the smaller retail outlets who were not allowed to open whilst they allowed the supermarkets to continue trading. Essential items only they said. Essential shops only they said. The big problem with that is that essential items cannot be defined as some things, a luxury to some, are essential to others. Thus began the totally confusing daily announcements from Downing Street that still seem to be as clear as mud. I have been waiting for them to tell me I can only shop when it's raining or if the wind is blowing in a north-easterly direction. It may still happen as the situation worsens and a second spike hits us all like a sledgehammer.

Seriously hassled mothers, close to mental breaking point, have a right to insist that the sweet shop and its contents are a necessary shop if it stops demanding toddlers from sending their parents up the proverbial wall. Purchases from a sweet shop could be classed as an emergency pack, a mental first-aid kit, and it's an argument that would be difficult to deny.

Was it wrong to close down shops that flogged ice-cream that reduced the decibels of young children? Was it wrong to close down shops that provided the treats that went into lunch boxes when the kids finally returned to school? When rules and regulations should have been written in black and white everything has been written in grey and nobody has the slightest idea what is right or wrong. It's all a bit of a pick and mix, similar to the sweet shop's offerings themselves.

There are very few bespoke sweet shops around now and I have a sad hunch there will be even fewer by the time I have finished writing this book, what with the new shopping technique of visiting the one big place under that one big roof. I, personally, happen to think that sweet shops are indeed essential outlets that should have been allowed to stay open, but that's because I have noisy neighbours with noisy kids who would have quietened down if the parents had been given the opportunity to shove ice-creams in those small faces.

So, although it is a shop I have rarely frequented, even during childhood, I have to say I shall miss the sweet shop if the last ones, hanging by a thread, never manage to re-open their doors with any form of gusto. It will, in turn, become a worry to parents and dentists alike as the future looks ever bleaker as less sugar is consumed.

Chapter Fifteen – The Travel Agent

I don't ever recall seeing a travel agent in the high street during my schooldays, probably because we, I mean my generation and not just my family, never went anywhere further than Cornwall down in the west country or up to Great Yarmouth in Norfolk. We didn't need to acquire bundles of brochures, we just climbed aboard a train and went. Flush families went for a fortnight and those with shallower pockets went for a week, until ten days became a happy compromise between the two.

Billy Butlin opened the first holiday camp way back in 1936 but unfortunately, four years later, many of our captured soldiers spent time in a completely different camp, which took the shine off the idea for a while. That first camp opened way up in Skegness, too far for my family to even think about travelling to. The second, just a year before the outbreak of The Second World War, was in Clacton, Essex, far closer but still not that enticing. After the war they were popping up all over the place as they became more and more popular with the working-classes who had never set foot out of the country before, other than in uniform. Now only three Butlins camps remain, in Skegness, Minehead and

Bognor Regis, but they served their purpose in years gone by. Then came the package holiday boom and that's when the colourful brochures started appearing in the high street. The big supermarkets tried cashing and crashing into that industry too, but it turned out to be one of the rare instances where they failed.

It must have been a flight of sheer fantasy to walk into such places and dream of exotic beaches in far flung lands and walk out with a brochure full of pictures of places you were unlikely to visit. Well, that's the way it is right now as the whole idea has turned full circle.

Many years passed before the thought of a flight down to The Caribbean entered our minds, to say nothing of our bank balances. As the 1970s came upon us British people flocked to Spain to escape either the rotten British weather or the British police. I certainly don't remember such flamboyant escapes happening when I was young kid. It was a sandy British beach for the family and a safehouse in Essex for the criminal.

I cannot say with any great authority who the first high street travel agent happened to be because, for reasons just mentioned, I never took too much notice. Lunn Poly seems to ring a bell because I remember their TV commercial. I think we all now know that Thomas Cook got the ball rolling but companies like Lunn Poly and Thomson Travel seemed to take the lion's share as I moved into my teens. I only say that because I cannot remember a Thomas Cook shop as a child. Neither can I remember the names of my first neighbours who flew to Spain at the start of the package holiday charge. It may have been Mr and Mrs Strange, maybe not, but they were a big-headed couple who boasted a fictitious life-style way above their station. They had a car and a caravan to pull along as a sign of their decadence. Yes, Mr and Mrs Strange fitted the bill.

The weather has been truly glorious of late and yet, despite that, the roads have been bereft of any caravans, trailers or motor homes on our empty roads. That may well be considered a plus for many at a time of so many minuses. It's only a minor plus against the huge negative of thousands ignoring government orders to stay vigilant by driving down to the coast under the clear blue skies and cramming together, like washed-up sardines, on beaches. It's all very well them sticking their two fingers up at the authorities but, right now, a nasty piece of work is sticking two fingers up at them, behind their backs, and it can only end up in tears. I understand pets being taken for walk and family members just six feet away from long-awaited hugs, but to see thousands not heeding the warnings and lying on the beach side by side, none wearing any form of protective clothing is utter madness. There are hundreds more swimming in the sea with next to nothing on before queuing next to other scantily-clad types for ice-creams. Thousands upon thousands within touching distance of each other, defying the second vicious spike. I sense they've lit a firework but haven't stood clear, all because their package holidays abroad have been cancelled.

The first package holiday, as we know them today, was organised by Horizon Travel who sent people off to enjoy the sun in Corsica in the late 1950s, their only rivals being British European Airways who offered a similar excursion to Valencia in Spain. They were the pair responsible for the mass summer exodus that has become so much a part the British way of life. Now the skies are empty, apart from the songbirds and butterflies, and nobody is going anywhere.

All aeroplanes sit neglected in airports, airlines are going out business and thousands of airline staff and members of the travel industry are now out of work. Summer holidays we'd booked at the turn of the year seemed a long way and safe as we loaded up our credit cards shortly before we first encountered the deadly invasion. True to say that none of us believed for a moment we would still be struggling so many months later, but struggling we are and a trip to the beach against orders will not make things better, quite the opposite. It will be a tough time for the countries overseas that rely on tourism, but we can't, as a nation, come to their rescue when we have enough problems of our own.

The advent of the travel agent corresponded with the invention of the thick felt-tip pen. Without those big red and black markers there would have been none of those multitude of special offers that dominated every window of every travel agent in every high street. There were special offers thrown at us in all directions and if we'd read them all we would all have gone down with a migraine.

Then came other attractions such as Disneyland and wonderful cruises for those who had retired. The big white cruise ships, those floating palaces of decadence, were originally built for old age pensioners or lucky people who had come up with eight score draws on the football pools. Your everyday Joe Bloggs never considered a cruise to be financially viable. Prices eventually fell and the cruise industry raked it in by the millions as more and more put their sea legs to the test. That is now well and truly in the past. Suddenly, the ships have hit the dreaded iceberg. Some are floundering in mid-ocean full of stranded passengers who didn't mind for the first few weeks they couldn't dock anywhere, but are now desperate to get back home. A life on the ocean waves is all very well, but not the rest of your life on the oceans waves, that wasn't the lyric of that jovial song. Those cruise ships remain moored up wherever they happened to find themselves on a given day and Mickey Mouse is banned from welcoming little ones to his kingdom

Recent events have put paid to all aspirational and inspirational distant travel for the immediate future. The population can't even pop down the road to visit their families in the usual manner, let alone take a flight to a warm beach and beautiful blue sea. Those British resorts are supposed to be out of bounds too and, to add salt to the wound, the British weather has gone tropical and we all feel like roast potatoes sitting in an oven as we idle in our gardens and on our balconies soaking up the rays with nothing better to do.

Many of us have taken up gardening, myself included, so, as expected all online suppliers have run out of runner beans and tomato seeds as we all suddenly feel we have developed green fingers.

I have discovered something quite erotic about growing vegetables. The more you pay them attention the more they seem to respond and I have a hunch my runner beans will be pole dancing before too long. I'm actually finding the plants rather attractive too which is worrying. I'll have to eat them all shortly and that may hurt, more them than me, but it will hurt just the same. I wave to them every morning and they wave back in the calm breeze as our friendship grows. Oh dear, Cannibal Nectar is on his way.

The holiday offers have disappeared, no special offers available in shop windows or in newspapers as the travel industry grinds to a longer halt than anyone expected. Airlines have admitted things may not return to full normality for four or five years and hoteliers in every country are going bust. I'm not saying for one moment there could ever have been a right time for this to come and hit us, but for those two industries it is certainly the wrong time.

The holiday and travel industries obviously generate most of their income in the summer months, but this particular summer all thoughts of a holiday at home or abroad have been written off. The whole year sort of hasn't happened. Millions are now unemployed and can't even think about taking a holiday, home or abroad.

Many people are saying the whole, sad affair has brought the country together. I understand the upbeat claim yet there are so many whom we have lost in this Third World War battle and there are many others who are now far apart from their families and friends. It isn't the time to think about a holiday for any of us right now, not just the unemployed. Britain, along with the rest of the world, is at a virtual standstill as we watch the number of casualties escalate with medical staff stretched to their limits and beyond. None of us escape the attack as we all know someone who has been stricken down. I doubt if Stephen King could have dreamt up this scenario.

Chapter Sixteen – The Pet Shop

I've never been a fan of pet shops. As a child I was never one to stroll into such a place to marvel at the rabbits and the guinea pigs. For a start, I didn't like the smell and more significantly I didn't particularly like rabbits and guinea pigs. Even so, I hated the thought of them encaged in a shop waiting to be claimed as a birthday present for a young child who may not have looked after them. Animals belong in the wild, just like I did until recent global events changed my lifestyle, probably forever.

Every pet shop seemed to have a smell of four-legged incontinence and sawdust, another aspect that prevented me from going through the door. I remember one of the very few times I visited such a place. As I walked in a loud doorbell clanged and all the budgerigars and parrots went completely mental, frightening the life out of me. Lizards nudged a quarter of an inch with fright and mice scampered for cover. The shopkeeper would appear, strolling down from the back of the shop holding something or other that struggled to break free.

I hate to see birds in cages, rabbits in hutches and reptiles in glass cases so small they cannot move. It just isn't right. I used to wonder if the owners of pet shops had some kind of macabre, vindictive attitude towards animals that induces some kind of pleasure in seeing them all banged up so alien to their natural habitat.

Pets come in all shapes and senses. I recall the time when a lad called Hoskins brought his pet snake into school one day and emptied the classroom in five minutes flat. He hid it in his desk, with the lid flapping up and down until the teacher walked in and all hell broke loose.

Snakes were never designed to be a pet, a statement that confirms to you I'm scared stiff of the things, probably because they are covered from head to tail in tattoos. I really don't like the way they keep poking their tongues out at me, daring me to retaliate, which I am far too scared to do, so they would be wasting their time.

Why own one? You can't take them for a walk, they can't jump and catch a ball and you can't teach them to sit up and beg for a tasty morsel. What's the point of having one? If you own a baby one that shakes its rattle at you you're in serious trouble. The other thing about snakes is some of them can give you a nasty bite, and those that don't bite can hug you until they have broken your rib-cage. That doesn't sound like a particularly friendly pet to me. I've often wondered if a poisonous specimen would die if it bit its own lip. I've seen exotic dancers wrap them around their necks as some kind of erotic accessory. I disagree. As far as I'm concerned it just goes to prove their mums couldn't be bothered to knit them a scarf.

I've never understood how snakes escape from their owners. The ones I've seen never bloody move an inch and yet you occasionally hear of one that has gone missing. How do the dreaded things escape? They can't jump out their cages, climb through a window and leg it. They can't open a door and shoot off when nobody is looking. Maybe when their owners are out they smash the glass of the cage, slither their way to the kitchen and escape through a cat-flap. I know it happens a lot in America, but lots of nasty things happen in America that don't happen here, thank heavens.

If such pet-lovers adore their shape then why not adopt a homeless worm? They're much smaller and far less aggressive, and yet you never hear of anyone who had a pet worm. Fair enough, they are not playful little things that learn tricks or curl up in a ball by the fireside, but they're a darn sight easier to feed and much cheaper as you don't need to go to the pet shop to buy one. It's easy to just dig one up from the ground, fend off a vicious starling that wants to fight you for it, then take it home and sling it in an empty buttery spread container. Do you see how I'm trying to keep up with the times? Buttery spread indeed. It used to be called margarine but that seems to be a word of the past. I feel sorry for worms. You never see an attractive one or an ugly one, they're just worms. It must be so boring not to be attracted or attractive to the one slithering next to you in the dirt. I can't imagine their lives have changed as much as mine this awful year.

Another friend of mine had a pet frog called Dennis and I wasn't too struck on him either. I wouldn't say I hated him to the extent I would have severed the poor thing in a way that French chefs find acceptable, but I couldn't envisage him sitting on my lap the way my cat Monty did as I watched television. My friend kept Dennis in his trouser pocket and it wobbled up and down, a most disconcerting action for any girl he was chatting up in the school playground.

Pet shops seem to sell endless quantities of unnecessary clobber. There are dog collars, presumably stocked for budding vicars, rubber bones, stupid contraptions that enable you sling a tennis ball a few hundred yards in a park, currently nor a socially acceptable thing to do, and wheels that allow hamsters to think they're having a ride on some tourist attraction on the banks of The River Thames. And all of that is just for starters.

Let's begin with cats. We loved our family pet Monty and we had him from a kitten. He became house-trained by making him relieve himself in one of mum's old cooking trays filled with shredded newspaper. It worked a treat. We never had to go to a pet shop and buy eco-friendly bags of cat litter, something or other that resembled rabbit droppings for a fiver. Shredded pages of The Daily Mirror was good enough for Monty and never once did he crap on the carpet of our living-room and it made good use of a

Daily Mirror. When he wanted to go out he made a cat noise and when he wanted to come back in he made a similar cat noise outside. We didn't need to go and buy a twenty-pound cat-flap. He knew the rules and he obeyed. The other strange thing I remember about Monty was that he was never ill, just as well because I don't recall too many veterinary practices in the 1960s and we couldn't afford to visit them anyway if they had existed.

My dad always said he would never take an animal to a veterinary practice until the vets mastered their job and stopped practicing, probably the very same reason he never went to the dental practice either. Yet another profound statement from my family bard, a man never short of words yet short of logic.

The dog lovers rarely needed to drop into a pet shop either. Tins of dog food and boxes of Winalot could be purchased at the grocer's as part of the regular food shop and if owners ran out of such provisions they could give their pets the leftovers from their dinners. It wasn't rocket science.

If you owned a dog and decided to let it join you in a stroll along the high street you couldn't possibly take it into a pet shop without it becoming mortified at the thought of re-housing, so they had to be tethered outside with a threat of abandonment. I always thought it funny that all pet shops had 'no dogs allowed' signs on their doors, or was I missing something?

On a far more serious note, as I sit here wondering in my self-confinement, I spare a thought for the homeless members of our society who have nothing but a loyal four-legged friend to keep them company. It hurts me inside at normal times when I see them in shop doorways trying to keep warm with their friendly companion by their side. I wonder how they are doing right now? It's a humbling thought that makes me realise there are so many struggling people out there, far worse off than me, so I need to pull myself together and stop feeling so sorry for myself. That four-legged chum will have no idea what's going in the world today and yet it will wake up each morning with a wagging tail and a look of affection, a sobering thought.

Back to the pet shop and the aquarium section of tropical and cold-water fish, terrapins, crabs and things that stick to the glass and don't move, whatever they are. It's a myriad of panoramic wonder to tiny eyes but let's be honest, wouldn't we rather see the little lives swimming around in their natural environment? Like the dogs they have no idea how devastating our own lives are. Admittedly, fish tanks in a pet shop offer a better future to their inhabitants than one in a posh restaurant, but they still give me a feeling of human brutality. It isn't just the way they have to live, bored out of their colourful skins, but the fact they have to swim around stupid objects such as miniature, derelict castles, deep-sea divers and wrecked boats, an insult to them, regardless of their intellects.

An even sadder thing for me about a pet shop is when they try desperately to enter into the spirit of Christmas by selling the most ridiculous of gifts that no animal would have requested on their list to Santa if they'd had the ability to write. They sell Christmas stockings full of stuff that bears no resemblance to anything in an animal's life. Cat treats, sultanas to you and I, beautifully boxed and an imitation mouse made of felt. Monty hot-pawed over to the local allotments when he fancied a mouse, not an imitation bright red thing, but a real one. Unfortunately, if successful, he brought it back home to show off his trophy.

We gave Monty a bell once and, petrified of the thing, it sent him round the twist, so much so that if there was boxing on the TV he would hide under the sofa every three minutes. Mince pie flavoured cat food? A red dog collar with flashing lights? The poor thing would be going for a walk, not reversing and emptying the dustbins.

Analysing the purpose of such a shop is a fine example of contradiction. They sell mouse traps and little toys for mice who survive the traps. They also sell mirrors for budgerigars that don't have hair to comb and cage hoods for parrots that are not encouraged to look at themselves or anything else. They sell dog leads and balls to throw for a dog who isn't on a lead. They sell wild bird-food for tame birds and ant powder that stops wild birds enjoying their natural nourishment of ants, plus crickets for lizards and spiders that most lizards would probably prefer. Then there are the flea collars. Dogs had posh leather ones and cats had to go with cheap linen versions. Dog baskets were made of material and cat beds were made out of the stuff with which they used to make wicker baskets. Oh, such a mish-mash, no wonder the place didn't really interest me. Once upon a time they even sold cats that chased mice and dogs that chased cats. I cannot imagine they all lived in perfect harmony as they waited to go to a loving home.

Thankfully it isn't possible just to walk into a shop and buy a dog these days, as both potential owner and animal have to be vetted before coming together. That's one of the few sensible aspects of this strange time as such rulings have become stricter.

The recent bacterial attack on the world has affected the animal care homes that look after those in wait for a better life. With social distancing it isn't possible to walk around the kennels to see which poor soul takes your fancy, meaning that such places are currently full to the brim with those living in hope. It all paints a pitiful picture of what has happened, not just to us humans, but all creatures great and small.

Dog-walking in parks has been heavily sanctioned and even the well-behaved pets can't be let off the lead to have a good run around or have a good clear-out in the bushes. No animal could possibly understand such rulings, or why their owners have suddenly adopted a stricter discipline upon them. It just isn't fair and it's a great shame that the flow of animals through such animal centres had ground to a halt like most other things. It would be wonderful to see many of the pet shop inmates in their natural habitat once again, no longer caged or tethered. It may be another case of the bad leading to good.

I was about to close my pet shop chapter when I suddenly had a vision of a pet gerbil my sister owned. She'd always wanted one as she thought they were such cuddly little things, never realising they were nothing more than desert rats that, in the wild, buried their heads in the sand in a similar way to an ostrich, a creature with similar habits but longer legs. In the wild they fall victim of the red fox. In a domestic situation my sister's gerbil fell victim to Monty who was having no such creature on his patch. She cried for a couple of hours before realising that messing around with my mum's make-up was far better than fun than keeping a gerbil. She didn't speak to Monty for days and he didn't even notice.

Chapter Seventeen – The Post Office

Postmistresses used to be scary people whom you never dared to fall out with as they seemed to wield some kind of authoritative power. Postmasters acted like strict headmasters who always seemed short of time and patience, huffing and puffing as they went about gathering and handing over your requirements through a window that resembled a railway station booking office before the days of Perspex screens. I don't have any idea why I have such visions in my head of the pair of them as it may well be an unfair appraisal but I always walked into a post office with trepidation.

It may well be known as The Royal Mail these days but I've never seen The Queen, or any other members of The Royal Family, nip out to post a letter or renew their TV licences, so I'm sticking with the post office as it's a more accurate title. Come to think of it, I've never even seen The Queen, oh and I mean in real life. I know what likes like, a stamp on legs.

There were two kinds of post offices, the placid rural village variety and its hectic high street counterpart. I knew nothing of the countryside version until much later in my life, being brought up in our capital city, so my recollections vary depending on how far my brain decides to take me back. The modern type has been a redundant factor in my life for months now and yet I cannot deny it plays a significant part of modern lifestyle. We now queue with precision for anything and everything and had the post office never been invented none of us would have learned the skill of irritating and unnecessary queuing and developing it into a good old British art-form admired around the world. That's why I feel we should be thankful to the post office, where it began for all of us.

When we were allowed to travel abroad our holidays always began at the airport, being part of a queue that slithered backwards and forwards like a snake until, an hour later, we reached the check-in desk to meet the nice lady who wore too much make-up.

I'm not just talking about the last few months, but more through the years that have passed, the post office has been a unique experience that set us up for this painful pastime. If all the shops in the high street were completely empty and the sound of footsteps did not echo on our pavements you could still guarantee to find a long queue in the post office. Big post offices had as many serving windows as supermarkets had check out tills and yet it counted for nothing. If there were four serving windows then only two would be open. If there were twenty-four such windows only five would be open. Supermarkets adopted the same trend to keep the queuing tradition alive. Even in these troubled times it's rare for all tills to be manned. Ten tills could usually boast five closures.

Queuing has taken on a new slant recently what with masked customers and Perspex screens, but it all began, as a kind of apprenticeship, with the long waits at the post office.

I can't seem to recall any reason why I went to a post office as a kid as they never sold a thing that interested me. The only things that enter my head are National Saving Stamps. What the hell were they I hear you ask? They looked like postage stamps and they were a way of saving up, an early version of a Christmas or a thrift club that are around today. They were an insipid green colour and they sported a picture of a five-year-old Princess Anne with curly hair similar to the kid in the Pears Soap advert. By all accounts they'd been around for many years before, founded in 1916 as a means of raising money to continue the fight in World War One.

I seem to remember, if my history lessons were correct, income tax came into our lives for the same reason when, in 1799, our Prime Minister of the time, William Pitt The Younger, a strange name as he is no longer with us, came up with the wonderful idea of our ancestors having to fund our attendance in The Napoleonic Wars. I'd like to remind HMRC that particular war has now ended and so it may be the right time to abolish income tax and give us all a break. Come on guys, a joke's a joke. It's nothing more than a hindrance to us all and it would stop pop-singers and rock stars moving to America. I digress yet again.

The post office has never been much more than an opportunity for old people to gather and moan about life, or what's left of it, as they wait to collect their pensions. It's also the place where we acquired a passport application form when we were able to travel, car tax and driving licence application forms when we were allowed to drive and TV licence purchases when we could all be bothered to buy a TV licence. It seems the post office is grinding to a halt in terms of importance as such things have become surplus to our requirements as we aren't going anywhere anytime soon. We bought stamps there before the arrival of the email and postal orders before the days of direct debit charges, so as queuing in our daily lives grows ever longer I think the life of the poor old post office grows ever shorter.

The queues will now be with us forever, a bonus for those old people who want to continue moaning about things they can no longer grouse about in the doctor's surgery, but I can't say the same for the shop that invented them. It's such a shame that one of our great high street institutions is in danger of extinction but it may well be the case when the world moves on from its current dilemma and changes in communication continue. Yes, there will always be Christmas cards and presents to post but even that tradition is fast becoming a thing of the past what with ecards and online shopping. My friend Chas became a postman when he was made redundant from his job as a draughtsman. It wasn't what he had planned but he insisted that being a postman was better than walking the streets.

White vans now turn up at our homes with more regularity than the old-fashioned postie and so the future looks bleak for the weary post office that began life way back in 1660 as the good old GPO, the General Post Office. I think their letter of redundancy may well be in the post.

Chapter Eighteen – The Stationers

I loved the stationers. It had to be my favourite shop when a schoolboy. I felt so grown up when I walked in the place, as if I were about to finally do something rewarding with my life. I stared in wonder at the assortment of notebooks and pens that I didn't really need yet still found compelling. It still confuses me that such a shop could be such a magnet to someone, such as myself, who didn't enjoy school and never did their homework. The shop obviously had a great effect on me as I will be bring my own personal lockdown diary up to date very soon. It's handwritten because I still have a passion for fountain pens and have a wonderful and various collection of bottles of ink.

The best way to describe the stationers is to simply offer you a list, a list that hopefully speaks for itself as each individual item conjures up its own memory.

Let's begin with coloured paperclips. They came in tiny transparent boxes and were multi-coloured little gems. There must have been a hundred of them lying in wait and yet none of us used more than five or six before we lost interest in them and moved on to a stapler. There were coloured rulers for the young and slide-rules for the older student. There were pencils with rubbers on the end, diaries, greetings cards, daily planners, pencil sharpeners, wrapping paper, brown paper for parcels, Sellotape, and small bottles of different coloured inks. I marvelled at them all even though I didn't need a single one of them.

There were so many objects of interest found in the shop, one such item in particular had its very own individual, secondary items to be found within. That tin was known as a geometry set, something that contained numerous objects, most of which were a complete waste of time, even though they were good to have. Let's lift the lid and take a quick browse through these unwanted things.

To begin there was a compass in which a pencil had to be fitted into, even though the pencil flopped around and drew circles with bumps on. Then came a set of dividers, the first offensive weapon any of us owned in our youth. What were dividers? For those too young to know anything about them they were pointless pieces of apparatus that had two points. They are used, and have been used for many centuries, by mariners plotting charts and measuring distances between two points, but they never had such an important use at school during our geography lessons. It was far more fun to use them as a weapon to inflict pain on the arms of gullible kids who didn't have the courage to respond.

The protractor, a strange plastic object, a crescent shaped, half-moon thing etched with 180 black lines, too close together to offer any form of accuracy. They were an aid to draw a line at a certain angle, an impossible task for an unsharpened pencil. A schoolfriend of mine discovered they were useful for picking locks and breaking into sheds, so at least they were of some use.

Beneath a totally irrelevant stencil for drawing laboratory equipment that fitted neatly in the lid of the tin, sat two set squares, one pyramid shaped with 45 degree angled sides and the other called a 30/60 that looked far more lop-sided.

The final object, apart from an emaciated ruler that wasn't even six inches long, we called an eraser, the rubber as it used to be known. They comprised of a white end for pencils, the other coloured end being known as an ink-rubber. The unfortunate things about ink-rubbers was that they never rubbed anything out. They were like lumps of sandpaper and all they did was leave a hole in the paper. I owned a geometry set for a short time, until my dad realised it held more tobacco than the standard Golden Virginia tin and forced me to hand it over under protest.

These days there is no great need for the old-style stationers because the giant megastores sell all the things the stationers once called their own. Envelopes, padded envelopes, self-adhesive envelopes, all kinds of envelopes with the exception of window envelopes that have seemed to die a slow death. Balls of string, labels, cash-books, tags for suitcases, so many items that involved a trip to the stationers were now readily available elsewhere.

Since my home imprisonment I have no use for any of the listed objects. Due to my isolation I have been unable to post anything to anyone due to my inability to get to a post office and buy stamps. Yes, the current disaster has affected correspondence in all its varieties, with the obvious exceptions of emails and text messaging, but the change had been looming long before this time.

The opportunity to write to your bank had long gone, along with most of the bank's staff. They could email you with all sorts of threats and suggestions, yet you had no opportunity to reply. No need for a writing pad there then. Letters became as unfashionable as home telephones, whilst understanding bank employees, who read your letters with compassion, had more or less disappeared at a rate faster than the closures on the high street. With no need to write letters to any person or company, because they weren't allowed, together with the chances of getting a reply being zero anyway, the need for any kind of stationery had become utterly pointless.

I don't have much time for banks and they don't have much time for me. My last correspondence from them informed me my account was outstanding and I felt so please with such a kind compliment. Other than that, we don't have an awful lot to say to each other. I used to call my bank manager for a chat before he had his phone taken away from him. He must have seen red, just like most of our accounts right now.

I'm certain a few threatening letters will find their way through our letterboxes in the next couple of months, but with no clear method of reply it isn't worth stocking up with that writing pad, envelopes, or new roll-tip pens. No point whatsoever. Threatening letters actually make me smile. Have you noticed that, no matter who they are from, there is no way you can write a letter back? Yes, they can send you a stroppy letter, but you have to reply by email as they don't have anyone in their offices with the ability or gumption to open a letter.

With fewer and fewer letters being written and notepads appearing on mobile phones, the small stationers and the post office do indeed face an uncertain future.

It will be a great shame if the traditional postman does end up walking the streets. Chas loved his job. Yes I know there are female posties too but back in the old days such a lady never existed in that occupation. The Postman wore a blue uniform with a large brass badge on the lapel along with a cap that made him think he was a sergeant in the military. He rode a bike, made two deliveries every day and whistled as he went about his rounds and always had time for a quick chat or a kind around with the boys. They never turned up in shorts and trainers, hoodies or quilted waistcoats with woolly red hats. That just wasn't the done thing at all back in the day.

Lonely people had at least three visits a day. Two from the postman and one from the milkman who, funnily enough, seemed to whistle the same tunes as the postman. Even the local copper pedalled around on a bike, whistling away with not a care in the world, stopping off at the pub a quick pint with the lads after hours. Oh my, how times have changed through the years that have passed by in my life. The milkman is an object seen as rarely as a tartan woodpecker and coppers don't ride bikes anymore. That really isn't the kind of vehicle to help control the angry protest marchers in today's society. They'd let his tyres down and continue on their way.

Chapter Nineteen – The Toy Shop

The toy shop was the perfect outlet for spending birthday money. I still recall the excitement as I waited for the postman on my special day. He never delivered coloured envelopes back in the day but, although plain white things, they were of varying size and just as exciting. They made a beautiful noise as they fell from the letterbox to the mat in the hall before I witnessed the sheer joy of opening them all at great haste and sorting them into two piles, those that contained money and those that didn't. The ones without were placed on the mantlepiece and those with cash were given far more attention as I added up the grand sum, imagining all the wonderful things I could buy at the toy shop in the high street. A kind birthday wish was one thing, a few quid was another thing altogether.

There would be a pound note in one envelope, a ten-shilling note in another and even a few coins from the skinter relatives. The post office didn't mind delivering coins back then, not when they were to make the day of a young child. My sister used to steam the stamps off the envelopes and stick them in an album before she became interested in boys.

I can walk into that toy shop right now and see all the many wonders stacked on the shelves and the glass cabinet counter where toy soldiers stood alongside knights on horseback, cowboys and Indians and rubber frogmen for the bath.

My own toy army always needed enlistments as I lost so many in battle. Some went missing behind tufts of grass, others were left at friend's houses and the occasional soldier was swapped for a football card to complete my set.

My oldest recruits were given to me by my mother at the time of The Queen's Coronation. They were hardly fighters as they came in a box, all holding musical instruments, along with a ceremonial coach pulled by four white horses, but they loved being next to my paratroopers and stretcher-bearers belting our marching tunes that none of the others wanted to hear particularly. A new birthday meant I could re-stock and maybe buy a long-awaited Dinky toy from the shelves to my left as I entered the shop. There was always room for a new truck, an army ambulance, a tank or armoured vehicle.

I ignored the shelving to my right as they were filled with model railway accessories and I never owned a model railway. I ignored the girly stuff too for obvious reasons. I wasn't interested in dolls or their silly clothes. They had no place in my military parade. Teddy bears? I don't think so.

If I'd been sent enough money I would buy another Subbuteo football team too. My friends and I loved playing the flick-football game on rainy days during the summer holidays. You could buy players, floodlights, groundsmen pulling rollers, referees, corner flags and white continental balls, so there was always plenty of ways to spend my new-found wealth in ten minutes flat. The players would be transferred for a chocolate lolly, not all this half a million pound a week stuff.

As my own children grew, I sadly lamented the passing of the toy shop in the high street. The world of toys had spread to the giant megastores and shopping for suck little gems had taken on a different slant. It was just as well that I had two daughters as model soldiers couldn't be found for love nor money, apart from on The Antiques Roadshow. Long aisles were packed with games and merchandise relating to blockbuster movies and the girls loved to wander backwards and forwards making their selections as I loaded up the credit card. I imagine it has been much the same for all parents until a few months ago.

My own birthday money handed over to the shopkeeper, I went straight home and played with my toys, a fatal error, when I should have put them in a safe (if not the safety) of a high street bank without ever having taken any of them out of their original packaging. I played with them in the garden dirt, put them in the bath to see if they floated, which they didn't, slung them out of windows pretending they were aircraft, which they weren't. Sometimes, I re-painted them to make them look nice and give them a new lease of life. How stupid was that?

Another fatal error occurred when I threw the boxes away the very day I opened them, never thinking every one of those boxes had a silver lining. I devalued my toys daily until they became worthless objects not worthy of consideration with regards making money in my later years. What on earth was I thinking of? Lots of fun and innocence is all very well but sometimes it comes at a cost as I am now finding out in my current moment of need.

As the financial strings tighten today to the point of strangulation, I wish I had looked after my toys well enough to sell them online and make some money at a time when I cannot work. My financial future, yours too, doesn't look too rosy right now. I've dented my savings during my first three months of lockdown and I could well do with my model soldiers to help win this Third World War.

We all had the same chance of becoming rich but sadly we enjoyed are various toys too much and down the tubes went our personal fortunes. We should have stared at them lovingly for ten minutes before placing them all back in their boxes and sealing them in a dark room away from the Sun while they became valuable over the ensuing fifty years.

For those far too young to understand my words and descriptions of old toys just go with it because it happened. London double-decker buses crashed into chair legs and collided with on-coming lawnmowers with dreadfully fatal outcomes. My generation were reckless rebels, possibly something to do with the influence of James Dean and because of that my collection of Dinky Toys, Matchbox Toys, model railways, Airfix kits and tin soldiers paid the price.

For people such as myself, an over 70s vulnerable burden on society, it's all far too late now, but our parents must never be forgiven for our current debts and lack of wealth. They were our first financial advisers and every single one of us has the right to feel very let down by their total disinterest in our growing up and financial stability through the last half a century. They knew about old age before we did. They had a run at it while we were still coming of age. They simply weren't interested and that's sad and, frankly, unforgivable. Nearest and dearest indeed, dearest being the operative word. I wish they were still here to get a good telling-off.

Other potential investments were at my tiny, innocent fingertips too, some far more unlikely than others. My Mr. Potato Head turned out to be a fine example. Remember him? A jacket potato with bits and pieces to stab into like some crazed terrorist. Mum and dad never told me how valuable he would become if I had kept him unassembled and packed away. He first appeared in 1952, a few years after me, as a box of detached, brightly coloured body parts and accessories like spectacles and moustaches that could be attached to a real potato I stole from the kitchen. The world's most expensive Mr. Potato Head, this is hard to believe but true, was featured in the Neiman Marcus catalogue, a specialist luxury department store based in Dallas, in

2004, and sold for over £6,000. Ouch. The same as my other toys, I should have saved Mr Potato Head, if not the potatoes. Come to think of it I could have planted just one potato all those years ago and let the natural process begin. Mr Smith and Mr Walker did and they made fortunes. I would own a thriving crisp company by now and crisps have definitely increased in popularity during these recent troubled times. They have become an essential part of my evening's entertainment during lockdown. I've even learnt to tolerate the salt and vinegar variety, something that would have never happened under normal circumstances.

I think of the young children today who have missed out on birthday celebrations in recent months and I feel so sorry for them. No birthday cake or party and no chance for their parents to get to the toy shop and buy them something to make their eyes open wide with wonder. Thank God they have endless games to play for hours on end on their tablets. They have far more different forms of home entertainment than I ever did but it is still so very sad. Young boys don't need toy soldiers anymore when they can manage their own international football teams and girls don't need to push dolls around in prams when they can take virtual reality trips around magical palaces, mounted on white unicorns. They can occupy their minds far easier than trying to write a book!

Chapter Twenty – The DIY Store

The whole country must be smelling of disinfectant and paint right now as so many households are getting on with tedious jobs around the house they have put off for years. There used to be a time when only The Queen thought the whole country stank of fresh paint, but now it's all of us. As if we don't have enough violent headaches to contend with right now without the smell of paint creating even more.

I have never claimed to be a DIY expert, but I have really come into my own recently, not just in the house but out in the garden too. What with all the paint I've had to buy, I've had more deliveries than a maternity hospital nine months after Christmas Eve.

Painting is definitely not my strong point or I would have smarter window-sills and frames. I can try to paint a picture with enthusiasm and yet painting a cupboard bores me rigid. I can make non-drip paint slide down a door quicker than a spider on roller-skates. During a less worrying time, when I would have been thinking of far better things to do, I would paint a cupboard or door without rubbing it down, priming or applying an undercoat and it still looked half-decent. With so much time on my hands now I seek the impeccable. Every single piece of wood has been smoothed down to an ice-rink surface and carefully prepared before applying the final gloss coat. I didn't even know what primer was, let along spending my hard-earned cash on the stuff. Undercoat? Yes of course I knew all about those tins, but none ever went into my own shopping basket because I just couldn't be bothered. Now it's a different ballgame. My house has never looked neater, but the ironic twist is that no-one right now is able to marvel at my meticulous efforts. House guests have become a thing of the past and I sense the whole place will need a make-over by the time I have permission to welcome my friends back round for a get-together.

Hanging wallpaper? I'd rather hang the person who invented wallpaper.

The modern DIY store is a far cry from the old-fashioned hardware shop of yesteryear and yet it is the one outlet, out of all the varieties mentioned in this book, where I admit it is progress for the better. Their delivery man has contributed immensely to my sanity and I have other plans during future months that will involve him returning. I will need varnish for my new garden table, wire to hold my runner-bean sticks together, a new lampshade for my guest room, just in the hope of better times to come, horrible black sticky paint for my front gate and I may need a ladder if I decide to re-tile my roof. Now I have mastered the fine art of DIY I have a feeling there will be no stopping me. Let's be honest, there's not much else to be getting on with. It is my new hobby, even if my options were limited. I can already play the guitar and piano to mildly acceptable levels, I've joined around fifteen thousand jigsaw pieces together from various boxes. I've cooked things I've never cooked before and I've watched numerous movies I never wanted to watch in the first place. Thank heavens for the DIY store and long may it survive.

Chapter Twenty-One – The Music Shop

As a young child I never realised the importance of the music shop and how it would play such a major part in my life. The old shop in the high street had a furniture polish smell exuding from the two pianos positioned each side of the shop doorway, my nostrils remember that well. I loved music as a child, to the extent I even gave it my all, singing my heart out, during school assembly while others kids were playing around or passing silly love letters to each other. I ignored all that nonsense as I belted out the fact that The Lord was my shepherd, even though not a single sheep lived within ten miles of my parent's place.

Having opened with such a paragraph you may be surprised to learn I hardly ever went in such a shop, mainly because it was littered with all kinds of musical instruments, none of which I could ever afford.

The other reason I gave the place a miss was because most of my visit to the shops was for mother, to buy food, so she would have been shocked to the bones if I'd walked in with a grand piano under my arm. I knew the shop was there, I often glanced in the window, but I never had the time to go in if I was going to get back home in time to play football for the school.

My first visit I remember well. My sister had joined the school orchestra and so she needed to buy a recorder, one of those dreadful instruments that make us all cringe when we think of their very existence, and I went along with her to get one of the wretched things. There wasn't much choice as they were a light-brown colour with a white mouthpiece and they all cost exactly the same. There were no cheap or expensive ones as they were all crap. There wasn't any point in her trying one out as they were identical, equally out of tune. I'm sure the man in the music shop had a deal going with the school because my sister also had to buy a recorder tutorial book, a boring collection of pages with the words to nursery rhymes and simple manuscript. The first few days after that visit were sheer hell as she tried to master the thing, emptying her spit from the wooden tube between each attempt of Bah Bah Black Sheep. Whatever the cost it had to be a complete waste of money. Just when I thought things couldn't get any worse she took up the violin, a time when Monty the cat thought about leaving home.

It isn't just me that wonders what the future holds. My neglected guitar hasn't see daylight for weeks.

Where did you go? I missed your tender hand
Where did you go? I didn't understand
I looked all around but I couldn't see your face
I lay here wondering why you never took me out the case

I used to play the notes while you sang the song
All the times we spent together suddenly had gone
I wish I knew what happened to you
I want to know where did you go?

Where did you go? I've fallen out of tune
Where did you go? I hope you come back soon
The way you tuned me up the way you polished me
The way I helped you sing in a complimentary key
Everything went silent not a sound was heard
Not a single note was played not a single word
I wish I knew my strings do too
I want to know where did you go?

Where did you go? you never said
Where did you go? Did you play something else
instead?
Together every time you tried a brand new song
One minute you were with me next minute you had
gone
Once upon a time I was a special piece of wood
Then you were gone and I never understood
I wish I knew that you'd come through
But now I know you had to go

Chapter Twenty-Two – The Car Showrooms

I have never been a petrol-head, a car enthusiast. My own vehicle outside the window where I now sit has not been driven for over three months and the lady in my satnav has thankfully been laid off. It hasn't been cleaned for three months either, it just sits there looking bedraggled and unwanted. Join the club Mr Motor- Car.

The new rules inflicted upon us are so confusing I can't be bothered to switch on the ignition. Where can I drive? Nowhere whilst in self isolation. What about shopping? I can drive to a supermarket for essentials. What are considered essentials? I've already covered that sticky subject. It's now changed to whatever I consider to be essential. Now restrictions are lifted a little, can I visit my family? Yes, but only if they live in walking distance or if I happen to know a high-ranking politician. Can I drive anywhere? Yes, I can drive anywhere in the country so long as I stay six feet from the person I am visiting. My car thinks I have fallen out of love with it and, through no fault of my own, that is exactly what has happened. It's such a shame I've gone off such things as the local car factory where I was born created so much employment in the area, including my dad and my Uncle Bill before he became a man of the cloth and started selling second-hand suits.

I have tried to fathom out why it has been announced by the government that the first retail outlet to be allowed to open is the car showroom. I repeat again, we don't need our cars right now, let alone a new one. We're all trying to save money best we can and I, for one, do not consider buying a new car to be essential. There isn't six feet between a car driver and passenger so I'm assuming that if I do fancy a new one, I cannot take a test-drive with a salesperson sitting next to me. What if someone I don't know, let alone trust, tests the car before me? Is it possible to drive a car safely with a face covering, mouth mask and rubber gloves? Is it right to even drive a car to see if my eyesight hasn't failed me since I last gave it a go? Do you know what? I just can't be bothered right now.

The area of London where I was raised invented the second-hand car and subsequently the second-hand car dealer too. I always thought the arrival of the second-hand car came before new ones turning up on our streets, mainly because nobody where I lived owned such a brand new, gleaming vehicle. New cars were only for show so most remained on the forecourt for months, seldom bought.

Our first family vehicle was a Ford Prefect, nicknamed a sit up and beg, due to its humpbacked shape. Like all cars of the time it was black, such was Henry Ford's demand. It had a few dents, but we were assured the previous owner, a widow who only took it out it twice, and drove very carefully. Second-hand cars were bought with such trust and scrupulous honesty. Dad bought our car from Terry Simpkins or Simpson, one or the other, a former amateur boxer of note. All dads in our neighbourhood bought their second-hand cars from Terry Whoever because if they went to another dealer Terry would go round their houses and beat them up. Terry apparently had over fifty fights in the ring and only lost once, to a bloke from Liverpool with an attitude problem, so nobody argued with Terry, it wasn't the cleverest of moves.

The Ford Prefect was so small compared to the bigger cars of today, so it was a bit of a squeeze to fit us all in when we went out for the day. Mum sat in the passenger seat with the road atlas and we three children just about fitted in the back at a squeeze.

Dad never passed his driving test, he didn't have to because he drove an army truck around the plains of Africa during the war and that made him exempt from any such trial. There were no such things as traffic jams or one-way systems, no motorways, and definitely no teenage boy-racers who threatened their own lives along with everyone else's. Driving was a sedate, thirty miles per hour occasion and dad wore leather gloves as he turned the starting handle to get the engine going as he dislocated his elbow.

Terry, sheepskin coat draped over his shoulders, would spend his days standing on the forecourt hour after hour, threatening people to view his stock. Whenever dad drove by in our car Terry would turn away and light a cigarette, although it may well have been a cigar. I never knew why at my age, but that Ford Prefect died about a year after we took ownership. One careful owner indeed. He never mentioned the other three not so careful owners. We were broken-hearted when the Ford went to the scrapyard. It was my very first bereavement of sorts and I took it badly, we all did, so much so that I didn't fall quite so much in love with the next car bought from Terry, another black one of course, an Austin Ten by name. The Ford Prefect hadn't even gone cold when dad parked its replacement outside.

Car showrooms, although rarely situated in the high streets of today, haven't really changed that much. There are numerous Terrys of the world walking you around lines of cars that, nowadays all seem to look very much the same. They've all had careful owners. Where do all these widows and vicars come from?

I remain somewhat surprised, however, they were given priority over other far more important outlets when the shroud of enforced imprisonment had eventually been lifted. Being allowed to walk a few yards to sit in a nearby home or garden and the opportunity to buy a new car didn't make any sense. There again, nothing is making sense to me anymore. I think I might buy myself a racehorse this afternoon. I hate horseracing and so it will offer me a challenge to take my mind off other things.

Dad used to enjoy a flutter on the horses. He took it too seriously. If a horse he had backed came in last he would write to the jockey and ask for his money back. Every moan ended with him saying the horse that pulled our milk-cart could have done better. We all betted on The Grand National, even though I wasn't too sure what The Grand National was. We just picked a name from The Daily Mirror and hoped for the best. Dad almost had an addiction for betting on the horses and he would have been the happiest man alive to see horseracing return at Newcastle racecourse after such a long lay-off. He would have had a flutter.

Chapter Twenty-Three – The First Four Months

Trying to ride a bicycle for the very first time is a scary experience. We all tried and fell off but kept remounting in the hope things would become easier. They did become easier. Our first days at school were scary too, until we made new friends and discovered it wasn't so bad after all. I feel very much the same about my self-imposed isolation and eventual lockdown. The big difference was it just didn't get any easier. We weren't trying to ride bikes or venture to school, we were facing a complete change of life as we knew it.

I have to admit I quite enjoyed the first two weeks. I knew I could cope sitting around, reading a few books and catching up on a few movies I hadn't seen. I felt like some kind of pioneer, putting myself up on the same level as Scott of The Antarctic. I didn't exactly lock my door and tell the world I may be some time, but even so, I ventured into the unknown with a weird kind of excitement. My family understood the situation too. I wouldn't be seeing them for a few weeks but that wasn't anything new as my job took me to the far-flung corners of the world on occasions.

When two weeks stretched into months I took a different slant on things. I'd never shut myself away for a month before, let alone two months and then three.

Like everyone else, I trod tentatively into an unknown territory, as though lions and tigers were hiding behind trees and bushes. Yes, things began to ease as more confusing statements echoed from an empty Downing Street. It had to be empty as it was in London and our capital city stood desolate apart from the odd cyclist or jogger determined to make it to the office regardless of how much they perspired over their desks.

After the four months of isolated torture things seem to be edging slowly to some kind of normality. It's now a time when schoolkids are returning to their places of learning. Well, some are, but once again the messages coming out of Downing Street are confusing in the extreme. It all depends what day it is and which ball they pull out of the lottery bag. One moment everyone can return and continues their studying, the next it will all be held over for another three months. Such a break in education is dangerous. I only bunked off school half a dozen times and I failed most of my exams at sixteen.

Shops have re-opened too as I make my way to the end of my story, but shopping as we have always known it will never be the same again. The queuing and the minimum numbers allowed into a shop at any given time will be so strange for us all.

Can you imagine the January sales, all that chaos as hundreds wait to barge in and buy a half-price televisions? The stampede of the multitudes as they send security-guards scampering for cover when the doors are unbolted. I just can't imagine four people rushing into a large department store in Oxford Street and going to war over a bargain in a huge box.

I've clung to my nostalgic memories throughout these pages, during my own four months lost, and I now realise how much I will miss the strolling round the shops at my leisure. I think back and smile at the shopping errands my parents sent me on, those character building expeditions that were such a pain. I went as fast as my tiny feet would carry me so I could get to the playing fields and turn out for the school football team. I think of the rancid changing room in the park where we were crammed tight together as we put on our claret and blue shirts. Young kids will never experience that feeling of team spirit and togetherness, being separated by yellow lines and circular stickers on the ground. Dads will be gobbing off on the touchlines behind face-masks, the only saving grace being they can't get within a few metres of a referee to call him rude names because their sons and daughters weren't awarded a penalty.

Unfortunately, I lost interest in football years ago, preferring the days when it was a sport and not a mega global industry and so I'm not too bothered about its return behind closed doors. The way my local team play they should be locked in behind closed doors anyway to be honest.

The six seasons will turn and things will hopefully return to even more normality but it will obviously be a very slow process. Six seasons? Autumn, winter, spring, summer, football and cricket.

Chapter Twenty-Four – The Future

The future? What future? Most authors know how to end a book before they even begin, but that luxurious scenario is an impossibility for me. I have no idea where or when this Third World War will end, consequently I have no way of completing this book with a clear route towards the approaching final page. It's well and truly out of my washed and scrubbed hands.

This has been nothing more than a diary of events that I wanted to put into print. It has been a massive help to my mental well-being and I hope it has helped you too. There must be tears of laughter alongside tears of pain and they are the kind of tears I tried so hard to find.

However, I end this diary of sorts it can be nothing more than the story so far, simply because this story will never have an ending. The unwelcome visitor to our shores, indeed our planet, has no intention of going away any time soon. There will certainly be no happy ending anyway, whatever the outcome, as we will think back on the days we are witnessing now, the sacrifices, the victims, the shattered dreams and broken lives. No, there can never be a happy ending to all this.

Yes, like any war there will be heroes, we already have thousands and thousands of them tending to the sick and the needy. There will be those who will look back and think they could perhaps have done more. There will be politicians who will need to step up to the plate and admit to their wrong judgements and there will be others who will admit to their stupidity for heading to the beaches at such a time. Unlike the great words of Sir Winston Churchill, we were never able to fight this particular battle on the beaches.

My intention, when I began, was to create just a speck of light at the end of what seemed an eternal tunnel, smiling in the face of adversity, just as I had mentioned at the beginning, remembering those who went off to war in our grandfather's day and yet still found time and space to sing songs that reminded them of home as they adjusted their tin helmets and smoked a fag. It has also given me an opportunity to furnish my creative juices as an alternative to mental vegetation. Other than that, dear reader, I can offer no answers to the doubts I have raised, none of us can do that, but if it took you away from the stark wilderness we now find ourselves in, just for a short time, I feel it was worth giving it a go. It has been nothing much more than that, but it has kept me occupied. I mean, you can only paint so many doors and plant so many vegetables.

I hope you read this at another less scary time, long after we are free from the shackles of this Third World War. This tells how it happened to be for millions of us who had to live such a nightmare.

I have enjoyed my own personal trips down memory lane. It was all so long ago and there have been so many changes to the retail landscape since the time I ran my first errands for my mum and dad. I knew change would happen. I mean to say, I'm no longer three feet tall and wearing short trousers.

When I was three feet tall
Early TV I recall
I watched in black and white back then
The Woodentops and Bill and Ben
When I was three feet tall
The world was not scary place
No faceless enemy I had to face
My father was an astronaut
And he also worked at Fords
My backyard it was Wembley
It was Wimbledon or Lords
Always playing with a ball
When I was three feet tall

When I was four feet tall
Cuba scared us all
Khrushchev versus Kennedy
We braced ourselves for World War Three
When I was four feet tall
They built The Berlin Wall
I edge into the grown-ups land
A land I didn't understand

When I was five feet tall
I saw the writing on the wall
The grown-ups who had spoilt my fun
I realised that I was one
Now I am six feet tall
I see the three and four feet high
Staring in my grown-up eyes
Searching for the answers
That I searched for at that height
Searching through the tunnel
For that little speck of light
All trying to survive
And thanking God we're still alive.

I end this book as confused and lonely as when I started it. The only contact I have made is with my past and it has made me realise how lucky I have been to have lived at such a peaceful time and at such an easy-going pace, until now. My parents lived through that monumental bundle against the Germans and the Japanese and, with the exception of a few skirmishes in far-flung outposts of The British Empire, I have lived through an easy time.

If The Second World War had never happened the film industry would have gone bust, so it had its good points I suppose. I presume the same can be said for what's going on right now. I bet someone, somewhere, is writing a book about the strange events that led us to The Third World War, so there will be a film next. I live in Salisbury and they've already made a movie about our two Russian visitors, or should I say tourists? This a far greater story of more epic proportions.

I'm off to try and survive the second, third and fourth spikes of this dreadful invasion by the faceless enemy. I end by wishing you and yours the best of health as we continue along this road with no map or Satnav. For the many of us who have lost loved ones there are endless memories to recall. This whole book has exposed my own personal memories and it has proven to be an essential therapy for me. I hope your own memories work for you too as you think back on the better times, when you laughed with those who can no longer laugh and you went to places where some unfortunate victims cannot visit anymore. Cling to those memories and they will eventually bring smiles to your faces. It certainly worked for me.

All we can do is hope we make it through to the other side. What is waiting for us on the other side is anyone's guess, but one thing is for sure, the world will never be the same again. As we continue to take on the enemy behind our masks it returns my thoughts to the days of The Lone Ranger on black and white television. He was masked too, trying to do good, and only had Tonto, the Indian Native by his side. We have each other and that makes me think, even in these dark days, we will eventually win the fight. If those two could sort things out then so can we, so let's just keep on hoping,

Many years ago I put the memories of my childhood into rhyme, how it all began for me in

Plaistow, in the East End of London and I think it appropriate to end with those very words to allow my story to end on a lighter note. For younger readers it is a history lesson that tells of how things used to be. Us older people often refer to the so-called good old days and just maybe they weren't so bad after all.

Plaistow through the bars of a cot
Plaistow through the eyes of a tot
Nappies damp as the whitewashed wall
Dad's money is standing in Newmarket stalls

Tiny trickling private parts
Pathetic strains and weak little farts
Trolley bus din and horse drawn carts
This is where life's journey starts

When I grow up I'll make good for sure
Let's hope there isn't another World War
Dubious Dames in half lit lanes
Feel in the dark for man's loose change

Stockinged legs unparalleled seams on
Snuggle up close to the sailors with jeans on
When I grow up I'll make good for sure
Just as soon as I'm told what this little thing's for

Plaistow through the eyes of a nipper
With a body no bigger than granddad's slipper
Terraced houses leaning into each other

Like whispering oldens or teenage lovers

National Health orange juice cod liver oil
Milk for Ovaltine just on the boil
Plaistow this little world was mine
My wardrobe dangling on the washing line

Plaistow through the eyes of a child
The stench of Docklands and brown and mild
Craving attention, screaming for love
Annoying the neighbours next door and above

"Doesn't he look like his dad" they all say
The same bloody dribble and public house sway
When I grow up I'll have a good look
Perhaps a draughtsman, more likely a crook

Plaistow through the bars of a cot
Plaistow through the eyes of a tot
Sister's getting married again
Fell for some bloke on a Fenchurch street train

When I grow up I'll get married an' all
Who? Depends if I'm little or tall
Plaistow through the bars of a cot
A tranquil landscape it's certainly not

Keep well, dear reader.

Printed in Poland
by Amazon Fulfillment
Poland Sp. z o.o., Wrocław